Comments from others on *Michelangelo: In the Footsteps of the Master:*

"This is a practical and interesting idea for a book. It should be helpful in many ways".
-----Dr. C. L. Joost-Gaugier, PhD. Renaissance art scholar

"Reading *Michelangelo: In the Footsteps of the Master* brings a real appreciation of both the art and the history of one of the world's most talented figures. Far more than a travel guide, but less than a full-blown biography, this book strikes a perfect balance to entice the reader to both see and understand the power of Michelangelo's work. Without this book, the seriously interested art student and traveler would miss many wonderful pieces. Altogether, this is a wonderful read for those preparing a trip to Italy, complete with careful directions for finding each site, or for the armchair traveler just wishing. . . . Time well spent!
-----Mike Koury, historian and publisher

"This book is educational without being overwhelming. It is a terrific illustration of the satisfaction one can enjoy and the unexpected surprises one may experience. The excellent appendix provides the comprehensive bibliography I will need to fulfill my desire to learn more about Michelangelo's life. I will be packing this book on my next trip to Italy to use the extensive list of places to see".
-----Debbie Larson, traveler and travel agent

Michelangelo:

In the Footsteps of the Master

with love to Mother

from Lauren

An Account of Michelangelo's Life and Art
for the Modern Traveler

Charles J. Washington

Happy Mother's Day 2008!

Published by Advantage Publishing
P. O. Box 881
Fort Collins, CO 80522

Publisher's Cataloging-in-Publication Data
Washington, Charles J.
   Michelangelo: In the Footsteps of the Master: an account of Michelangelo's life and art for the modern traveler / Charles J. Washington--Fort Collins, CO.: Advantage Publishing, 2001
        p.   cm.
   Includes bibliographical references and index.
   ISBN 0-9667775-1-4
   1. Michelangelo Buonarroti, 1475-1564.   2. Artists--Italy-- Biography.
   3. Art--16th century--Italy.   4. Italy--Description and travel.   I. Title.
     II. In the footsteps of the master.

N6923.B9 W37	2001	2000-135836
709/.2	dc21	CIP

Project Coordination by Jenkins Group, Inc. ● www.bookpublishing.com

05 04 03 02 01 ▲ 5 4 3 2 1

Printed in the United States of America

Dedication:

To Ruth, my best friend and my wife for more than 40 years. She is a great traveling companion who provided constant support during months of writing time. Ruth helped with recording the many details for the information and documentation on the research trip to Italy. She also did the proofreading on the the different drafts and revisions. She is in the picture holding up the blocks of marble in Carrara on page 44.

A man who has not been in Italy is always conscious of an inferiority from his not having seen what it is expected a man should see."

Dr. Samuel Johnson, April 11, 1776, as quoted by James Boswell in *Life of Johnson*, edited by R. W. Chapman. Third Edition, Oxford University Press, London, 1970. Page 742.

CONTENTS

CONTENTS

One may wonder why another book, this book, is written about Michelangelo Buonarroti. After all, hundreds of books have been written on the great artist, sculptor and architect who lived his life so fully during the Renaissance period in Italy. This book was written to meet a perceived need that I discovered as a result of a vacation trip to Italy in September of 1998. I discovered that I had missed seeing a lot of the places Michelangelo frequented and many places where his magnificent works still exist today. When I was in Italy, I didn't know everywhere to look. Which cities in Italy and which buildings housed his works that are available for observation today?

This discovery bothered me because I had no intention of going back to Italy and, therefore, I would not ever see the places and artwork that I missed. In looking for a book that would trace Michelangelo's footsteps and follow him chronologically from birth to death, I found there was no such book available. I asked many people and checked with many bookstores to no avail. When I inquired as to the interest level in such a book, the positive answers were unanimous. Aha! Other travelers, art lovers and history buffs all thought the concept was a good one in which they would be interested as a buyer and reader of such a book. Friends and relatives were very encouraging.

In deciding to evaluate the possibility of writing such a book, I found that I had many of the skills and interests needed to write the book. I was a history major in college and had taken courses in art history and architecture and I had done research on several artists for lengthy papers. In my ensuing business career, research was a cornerstone for my problem solving. Furthermore, I have a great interest in travel and in photography. Also, I have previously written newspaper columns and written a book on business issues, so I have some writing experience that would help me. When I looked at all these dimensions, I felt I had most of the ingredients needed in order to write this book on Michelangelo. Perhaps most of all, I had the passion for it!

I started researching the background on Michelangelo in March of 1999. In the following months, I read any book on Michelangelo that I could find. I searched used bookstores, new bookstores, flea markets and the Internet and bought dozens of used books, and some new ones, too. I found that there are not many used books in bookstores when you consider how many different books have been written on Michelangelo just in the last 100 years alone.

Apparently, people keep their Michelangelo books rather than turn them over to the second-hand outlets. When they learned of the writing project, friends loaned me books on Michelangelo from their personal libraries to help provide information. Books on the Renaissance and on related contemporary personalities, such as Leonardo da Vinci, Raphael, and the Medici family, were all eagerly collected and read. I was reading through these earlier books in order to find out where Michelangelo went, what he did there, when he went there, and where his remaining works still exist. I wanted a more comprehensive timetable and location list that were only partially covered in many existing books. Existing lists were not as fully developed and simplified as I desired.

As a result of this research, I found that I did indeed have to go back to Italy in order to see these places and works myself. I wanted to retrace the footsteps of Michelangelo and lay out the pathway for future travelers so they would not miss any items or places of interest like I did in 1998. I wanted to see where he was born, lived, worked and died. The 1998 trip included the more well-known works such as the David, the Sistine Chapel and the dome of St. Peter's Basilica. I discovered there was much more to see and many of the important sites were in Florence, nearby Tuscany and Rome. Therefore, I made a second trip to research these less well-known places for myself and to take pictures for the book. I spent 3½ weeks in Italy in November 1999. It was a good time to go; summer crowds were gone and it was before the Holy Year pilgrims descended on Italy in 2000.

I spent two weeks in Florence in a cozy two room apartment in Oltrarno that I found on the Internet. It was in a 350-year old building just a block from the Ponte Vecchio. Ten more days were spent in a delightful small hotel in Rome only three blocks from the Vatican. In order to get around to other nearby locations, I rented a car and made day trips out from Florence to key places such as Carrara, Siena, Bologna, Ferrara, Caprese, Settignano. Through the Internet, I engaged special art tour guides who were knowledgeable about Michelangelo in Siena and in Florence. We visited places known to Michelangelo where earlier artists worked that were a major influence on his work and are still today considered great works of art. These earlier artists include Masaccio, Brunelleschi, Giotto, Domenico Ghirlandaio, Bartoldo Giovanni, Jacopo della Quercia, Leonardo, etc. One can also include many of today's treasures of the Vatican that were available then to Michelangelo for inspiration. It is my hope that travelers, people interested in art of this period, students and history buffs will each get more from their visit to Italy as a result of reading this book before they go to Italy. It would be a great help to use it as a guide to set up their itinerary. I'm sure those who see Michelangelo's works in person will come to more fully appreciate what a great talent he was in his time and why he is still today considered one of the greatest multi-talented artists this world has ever seen. I am especially awed by what he could do with a block of marble. He chose his marble blocks carefully with a particular sculpture work in mind. His mission was to see the subject person imprisoned in the marble and free it with his chisel and hammer.

In summary then, this book traces Michelangelo's footsteps as described in the many existing books today, including his contemporary biographers, Vasari and Condivi. It provides the traveler, the art connoisseur, the student and the history buff with a comprehensive picture of where Michelangelo lived and worked and where his remaining works are still viewable. Some in Italy are not readily viewable such as the *Crucifixion of St. Peter* and the *Conversion of St. Paul*. These are in the Vatican in the Pauline Chapel and are not open to the general public.

This book is not an attempt to interpret Michelangelo's work in any way; other writers more qualified than I have done this in an outstanding fashion. See the extensive bibliography at the end of this book for these other authors. This book is simply designed as a guide to Michelangelo sites in central Italy with a few suggestions for making the trip easier and some information to make it more interesting.

Acknowledgments are due to the many people who assisted and encouraged me on the writing of this book. Their positive comments helped to maintain the motivation whenever they heard about the theme and how it would benefit travelers and those interested in Michelangelo. Special thanks go to Ugo Primadei, our tour guide in Florence who was very knowledgeable about Michelangelo and Florentine art in general. Special efforts he made to lead us out to Caprese were rewarding for both of us. Later, in the fall of 2000, he also assisted in learning about the process of obtaining some additional pictures from various art museums in Florence that I was not able to take on my trips there due to restrictions in place at the time. Thanks to the many friends and relatives who were supportive throughout the writing of the book. Thanks also to the people at Fratelli Alinari in Florence and their partner Art Resource in New York for assistance in obtaining the seven pictures used in the book that I did not take myself due to museum closures or restrictions. The head of Michelangelo shown on the title page is from the *Florentine Pieta*; the full picture appears in Chapter 14. Many thanks also go to the helpful people at the Jenkins Group and bookpublishing.com for their assistance and input that helped make a better book and bring it through the production stages.

I hope readers will obtain the expected benefits from the book. Any comments would be welcome.

Chuck Washington
Fort Collins, CO
March, 2001

Introduction:

If you have any interest in history, in the art of Michelangelo, and in the areas of Tuscany and Rome in Italy, you are about to embark on a journey that will be a highlight of all of your vacation trips. By learning what this book contains and by using it to plan your trip to Italy, you will know before you arrive what Michelangelo accomplished, when he accomplished it and where that work of art is today. You will be able to follow in his footsteps in Tuscany and Rome as I did in my trips to Italy. You can see the remaining works of Michelangelo without missing any due to not knowing where they are located. Most are available to the public for study and observation. A few art items are in private homes or Vatican apartments and these locations are not usually open to visits by tourists.

Your trip to Italy can be a focused trip on Michelangelo and his art or you can make Michelangelo's footsteps a part of a larger effort to see more of Italy. Either way, you will derive a great benefit from becoming familiar with the works of Michelangelo. The benefit will be the satisfaction of learning about Michelangelo and developing an appreciation for the greatest artist that has ever lived in my opinion. As you view his many artworks that still exist in Italy and consider the variety of the different media in which he worked, you will soon begin to appreciate his talent and find yourself in awe of his genius. As part of your trip, you will also be able to see the earlier artists in Tuscany and Rome, such as Masaccio and Donatello, who influenced Michelangelo in various ways. To study their art will help you to better understand and appreciate Michelangelo himself.

Michelangelo worked in sculpture and painting in his earlier years. His first known works were done when he was a teenager; they are marble reliefs of *Madonna of the Stairs* and the *Battle of the Centaurs*. His masterpieces were completed when he was in his twenties and thirties (*David*, the *Pieta*, and the Sistine Chapel). His efforts at architecture began with fortifications for Florence when he was in his fifties and culminated with the Basilica of St. Peter's in Rome which was completed after his death. His legacy in architecture alone is superlative for its design and later influence on other architects.

One can say that Michelangelo was a prime contributor to the Renaissance and at the same time was a product of the Renaissance. He lived from 1475 to 1564 in Florence and Rome. When he was just 13 years old, he started his apprenticeship in the most prominent art workshop in Florence and was discovered by the ruling Medici family at the age of 14. Lorenzo Medici, a great patron of the arts in Florence, took the young Michelangelo into his house and allowed him to participate in artistic training and experiments and intellectual discussions with the premier artists and scholars of the times. Later he was commissioned by several popes to do various works in Rome. Some of these popes from the Medici family he met as contemporaries when they all lived in the Medici Palace in Florence as teenagers and young adults. You could say he was very well connected.

To visit the places in which Michelangelo lived and worked throughout his life and career is to retrace the footsteps of one of the most remarkable men to ever have lived in Europe. Walking the same streets in Florence, stepping through the same doorways into the buildings that Michelangelo frequented, the churches, the municipal buildings, the houses, the palaces, the plazas, the public parks and Vatican areas, you will feel a great sense of history and be humbled by the experience. Many places are well preserved and very much the same as when Michelangelo was there. Many were spared and left undamaged by the various wars and battles that have wiggled their way across Italy in the last 450 years. Both civil wars and past wars of invasion did damage to some areas, but the many of the damaged locations were expertly restored to help maintain the feeling of the Renaissance period. Some buildings have been modified in appearance since Michelangelo saw them, but most of the modifications do not significantly destroy the character of the buildings as they existed during the Renaissance.

To view the various sites without being rushed, you will need ten days in Florence and a week in Rome. I was fortunate to be able to spend more time in both locations to do the research needed for this book.

November was a good time of the year to go because there were few tourists by comparison to the summer months of May through September. The taking of pictures was less cumbersome and more efficient without the crowds. Easier access to the museums and public buildings and lower prices for transportation and for apartments and hotels allowed for a more conservative budget without scrimping on the sights.

Starting in Rome or Florence makes little difference for the traveler, but by starting in Florence, it is a little easier to follow the chrono-logical development that Michelangelo went through. He was born in Tuscany about 2 ½ hours east of Florence and moved to the Florence area as a young child. His early development and training occurred in Florence and he always considered it home. In fact, he bought several homes in and around Florence. Whenever the stress got to be too much in Rome in later years, Michelangelo returned to Florence to regather his composure and put things into perspective. His tomb is in Florence which is where he stipulated he was to be buried. So Florence was and is today the central point with which to begin our trip following in the footsteps of Michelangelo. Another plus for using Florence as the center of focus for learning about Michelangelo is that most of the places to which he traveled (other than Rome and Venice) are nearby within a drive of two hours or less.

Driving to Florence from the Leonardo da Vinci airport in Fiumicino near Rome is about a four-hour trip including a stop for lunch. It is Autostrade driving most of the way on four-lane divided highways that are well-maintained toll roads. Leave the airport area going east on the expressway towards Rome. The signs mark directions very clearly. Proceed east for about 25 kilometers (15 miles) and get onto the GRA highway going north. This is a major highway that circles Rome and connects to many other autostrade highways for travel to anywhere in Italy. Take the GRA north and east to exit 8 which is SS-4. Go north on SS-4 for about 2 miles and find the Autostrade A-1dir going north to Florence (Firenze). Again, the signs mark it well.

A-1dir soon connects with A-1 which will take you all the way to Florence. You are now well out into the countryside so the scenery will become more open and hilly. Several tunnels and ancient hill-top towns are scattered along the way for variety and interest. At Florence, use one of four exits that will take you nearest to your hotel or apartment. If you are staying in or near the city center where parking is a challenge, check with your destination host ahead of time for parking arrangements. Visitor parking on the streets overnight is generally prohibited and parking in nearby neighborhoods is taking a chance without the proper window sticker that identifies you as a resident approved to park in that neighborhood. Tickets and tow trucks are plentiful and the police walk the neighborhoods looking for violators. Parking garages are available in most areas within walking distance of hotels and apartments, but be prepared to spend about 40,000 lire per day or more, even at weekly rates. Some of the better hotels have their own garages and may discount rates to their guests. Watch out for the on-street parking areas designated for fees; they are marked with yellow lines on the street and parking signs on nearby posts; they are well-guarded by an attendant who will collect your lire. These are ok for short-term parking for a few hours. Pay the attendant a deposit for your estimated parking time and get a slip of paper for the car window. Pay any remaining fee when you return; the attendant will usually be there when you return to your car.

You won't need the car for getting around in Florence proper, but it is a necessity for visiting the other towns on the itinerary. An alternate choice is to take the train to Florence from the Rome airport and then rent the car on a daily basis as you need it for the day trips around Florence. Once you have arrived in Florence and done some walking around to get a flavor of the city, you are ready to start in Michelangelo's footsteps. The streets in the city center on which you will be walking are the same streets that Michelangelo walked 500 years ago. They are not very wide, have few sidewalks or very narrow ones at best, and are choked with autos, trucks and busses as well as mopeds and bicycles and many pedestrians. You will find pedestrians walking in the street and cars driving and parking on the sidewalks. But that's part of the charm of Europe!

Buon viaggio!

CHAPTER 1

Michelangelo's Birth in 1475 and Early Years as a Child

Caprese: Birthplace

This book will trace the life of Michelangelo in chronological order. Travelers may follow in his footsteps chronologically or in random order as their schedule allows. By referring to the chronology in the Appendix, you will be able to identify where Michelangelo went, when he was there and what he accomplished there. Also, you will be aware of the remaining artworks that are available for public viewing without missing any through lack of information.

Michelangelo was born in Caprese in the far eastern reaches of Tuscany on Monday, March 6, 1475, about 40 miles southeast of Florence. His father Lodovico was appointed to a position as *podesta*, a combination of mayor, town clerk and police chief of the small town in the mountains starting on October 1, 1474. It was an appointment of six months so Michelangelo would not live very long in his birthplace. The house in which the Buonarroti family lived was a good solid home that the town allowed them to use as part of the compensation for Lodovico's administrative work. It is on the grounds of a nearby ancient castle high on a hillside overlooking beautiful valleys and mountain ranges rising up to 4,000 feet. Today there is a small museum in a nearby building and the birth home is part of the museum grounds; one admission fee covers both buildings.

The two-story stone birth home is well maintained. (See picture 1- 2.) Visitors can see the rooms where the Buonarroti family lived and the room in which Michelangelo was born. He was the second child and the second boy born into the family. His mother Francesca, even

Picture 1-1. The hilly countryside near Caprese, Italy, and
the road to the hilltop village where Michelangelo was born

though a young 19 years, was somewhat sickly and weak. According
to the museum attendant to whom we talked (with the help of our
guide), tradition describes how Francesca fell from the horse on which
she was riding when they moved to Caprese from Florence. She was
three months pregnant at the time with Michelangelo. Other than the
trauma of the fall and some bruises, there seemed to be no other injury
to mother or child. The traditional story told by the museum

Picture 1-2. The building in Caprese where Michelangelo
was born. This was the home provided to the family by
the town for his father's appointment as Mayor.

attendant goes on to say that the accident occurred on the church feast day of St. Michael the Archangel. Apparently, the young parents were very thankful for the miracle of their son surviving the fall while in his mother's womb, so, when he was born, they named him after the angel.

On March 8, just two days after his birth, Michelangelo was baptized in the small church at the foot of the hill below the house. Santo Giovanni Church is also a sturdy stone building that is able to accommodate about 30 people at a time (see 1-3 and 1-4). Our guide who showed us the way to Caprese asked the museum attendant to open the small chapel for us. Since it was November and few visitors were arriving, the chapel was kept secure. It is probably left open during the summer season for easier entry by the greater number of visitors. There is no admission for the chapel. The quiet and peaceful setting left a strong impression of serenity and closeness to nature.

Picture 1-3.   Santo Giovanni Church in Caprese where Michelangelo was baptized on March 8, 1475.

Picture 1-4. The interior of Santo Giovanni Church
in Caprese where Michelangelo was baptized in 1475.

Getting to Caprese will be a major challenge for visitors without a
guide who knows the back roads. With the help of our guide, we
drove south from Florence on the A-1 Autostrade that we used to
come north from Rome.   We left A-1 at the exit for Arezzo and traveled east through Arezzo to connect with highway No. 71. We took
No. 71 north towards Bibbiena and turned east on a rural road
towards Anghiari. At Anghiari we turned left and headed north on an
even smaller winding country road which climbed up into the mountains.   After looking at a detailed Touring Club Italiano map of
Tuscany, this route seemed about the shortest; with the mountain
ranges and valleys, it was scenic and relatively safe.

Driving time from Florence was approximately 2½ hours one way
with one stop for refreshments. It was an easy trip for one day with
plenty of time to look around Caprese and enjoy the small town's
ambience along with Michelangelo's first home and church. For this
trip, I would recommend visitors who don't speak Italian ask a guide
to accompany them if they drive because it would be very easy to get
lost on the mountain roads.   Another option is for summer travelers
to take a guided bus tour out of Florence to Caprese and leave the
driving to someone else. All of the other day trips out of Florence are

easier to accomplish than this one to Caprese. But don't miss it; Caprese is well worth the effort.

Settignano: Childhood Years

That afternoon on the way back to Florence, we left the Autostrade at the first Florence exit which was the eastern-most exit in order to stop in an area of what is now Fiesole. In past years the area we wished to see was known as Settignano. It was in this area that Michelangelo was raised until he was about ten years old. When Michelangelo was just a month old, the family left Caprese in April 1475 when Lodovico's term as Podesta was completed and moved back to the family home in Florence on Via dei Bentacordi. Because of his mother's poor health, the baby Michelangelo was sent to friends and neighbors in Settignano to be nourished by a wet nurse.

The Buonarroti family had a modest farm on the hillside in Settignano which overlooked the Arno Valley and Florence. The property had been in the family since 1427, possibly purchased by Lodovico's father. The family of the wet nurse lived nearby.

Picture 1-5. The original family farmhouse in Settignano near Florence. The tower and older section is behind the newer two-story addition.

Michelangelo spent most of his time with this surrogate family who made their living from working in the nearby stone quarries. Due to Francesca's poor health and the birth of three more sons into the family, it was deemed that Michelangelo should stay with the foster family in Settignano. He did visit the home in Florence occasionally for short periods, but he never really lived there with his growing family of four brothers. When he was six years old, Francesca's remaining health finally failed and she died in 1481. Michelangelo continued to live with the stonecutter's family in Settignano until he was ten years old. This area is about four miles due east of the center of old Florence. In Michelangelo's time it was a 90-minute walk.

The first ten years of Michelangelo's life were very formative for the young lad who was in all reality raised as a foster child. But by living with the stonecutter's family, he absorbed the basics of the craft and skill of stone cutting and sculpting that he was able to develop under later tutelage from other artisans. These formative years saw the planting of the seeds of greatness which were to blossom and be harvested in magnificent ways the rest of his life. One can only wonder, if Francesca had been healthy enough to raise Michelangelo, and if he did not have to live with the stonecutter's family, would he have developed his great sculpturing talent if he had lived his early years in the city of Florence.

Though the Buonarroti farmhouse in Settignano where Michelangelo lived in later years, when he wanted to get away from the city of Florence and its intrigues, is now a private villa and not open to the public, a visit to Settignano is still a worthwhile visit for an hour or so. Our guide was able to get permission for us to visit the Buonarroti farmhouse which today has been added onto and somewhat restored (see picture 1-5). We were able to walk around the grounds and imagine what it might have been like when Michelangelo visited there years ago. The basic house was very small and had a small tower attached to it. The tower is still there and several rooms have been added to make the small farm house into a wonderful villa with a fantastic view from the hillside.

Our hostess invited us into the first floor rooms to view the charcoal wall drawing attributed to Michelangelo. The subject is a mythological Triton or Centaur that was sketched on the kitchen wall by Michelangelo during one of his retreats from Florence. A few art-historian writers have described the drawing as a Satyr, but it is not often mentioned in the popular mainstream writings. In the early 1980's there was some publicity about the drawing and the state government was given permission to carefully reinforce and frame the drawing so it could be moved safely out of the house for public display. Afterwards, a Korean TV company came in and did a special program on the house and its priceless drawing.

You may be able to find an eight-page brochure prepared by Charles de Tolnay and Mario Salmi in second-hand bookstores and art stores that describes and photographs the house and the drawing as they appeared in 1980. The brochure is 11.5" x 15.75" in black and white. The drawing is shown on page 393 in the book *The Complete Work of Michelangelo* published by Reynal and Company in 1964.

Florence: Home at Last

In 1485, when he was ten years old Michelangelo moved to Florence to be with his family in the house on the corner of Via Bentacordi and Via dell Anguillara. (See picture 1-6). The house is still there in decent condition and is viewable from only the exterior; it is still used as a private residence. The family lived on one floor of the four-story building.

Picture 1-6. Michelangelo's home as a teenager in Florence

About this time, Michelangelo was enrolled in school by his father. This was really the first contact he had with any formal education. This part of his training lasted three years with his private instructor Francesco da Urbino. He managed to teach Michelangelo to read and write, but it was a struggle for both of them. Francesco could not get Michelangelo motivated to apply himself to learning how to read and write well for his age level. Michelangelo did learn the basics but he was more interested in drawing sketches and tinkering with stone-cutting and sculpturing tools. In his later years he did become a capable and prolific letter writer and poet. Nearly 500 of his letters are known today and other authors have written books about Michelangelo's poetry which he wrote throughout his life.

Michelangelo was mesmerized with the art that surrounded him in Florence. He spent all his spare time and some of his school time studying and sketching the paintings and statues that were left by the earlier Renaissance masters such as Masaccio, Donatello and Giotto. These were in churches and various public buildings. A few of these early drawings by Michelangelo from this period are known today. They are described in the next chapter. (See picture 1-7 for example).

Picture 1-7. The Brancacci Chapel at Santa Maria del Carmine where Masaccio created his masterpieces

His boyhood contacts were strongest among the young artists-in-training. His best friendship developed with a young artist six years older than himself, Francesco Granacci, who was an apprentice in the workshop of Domenico Ghirlandaio. Francesco remained a close friend of Michelangelo's throughout their lives. This early friendship resulted in the next phase of Michelangelo's artistic development. Up to this point, he had been pretty much self-taught. But this was about to change.

Michelangelo was born with a favorable horoscope.

In 1474[1], a son was born, under a fated and happy star, to Lodovico di Lionardo Buonarroti Simoni. The child was born on a Sunday[2], the 6th of March, in the eighth hour of the night, and the name he received was Michelangelo. Because he was inspired by some influence from above, the father thought he perceived something celestial and divine in him beyond what is usual with mortals, as was indeed afterwards inferred from the constellations of his nativity, Mercury and Venus exhibiting a friendly aspect, and being in the second house of Jupiter, which proved that his works of art, whether as conceived in the spirit or performed by hand, would admirable and stupendous.

From *Lives of Seventy of the Most Eminent Painters, Sculptors and Architects* by Giorgio Vasari. Edited and annotated by E. H. and E. W. Blashfield and A. A. Hopkins, Volume IV, Page 37. Charles Scribner's Sons, New York, 1896.

---

[1] According to the Florentine computation; by the Roman computation, the year was 1475.

[2] Actually on a Monday

CHAPTER 2

Formative Years: Training The Young Artist in Florence in the Medici Gardens

The Studio of Ghirlandaio

In the late 1400's Florence was the best place to live for anyone in Italy who thought they might have a career in painting, sculpture or architecture. As it turned out, Michelangelo had talent in all three art forms. Budding artists of the time could study the proliferation of artistic expression created by the masters who preceded them, some of whom were still living when Michelangelo was there as a youth. Many of these great works that Michelangelo studied are still there today for us to admire and appreciate. Refer to the appendix for a list of some of them. The most prominent artists of the time were Masaccio, Donatello and Brunelleschi, painter, sculptor and architect respectively. Wherever Michelangelo went in Florence, he was constantly seeing a treasure of some form of art. The same is true for today's visitor, too.

The citizens of Florence in the late 15th century and early 16th century knew they were living in a special time period for the creative arts. Their successes in trade and banking had produced a relatively high standard of living and several wealthy families like the Medici, Strozzi, Pazzi and Brancacci supported the artists with various commissions. The creative achievements of the past 150 years up to 1500 were widely recognized as the leading edge of artistic expression. Renowned artists from other cities, such as Leonardo da Vinci and Raphael came to Florence to study and observe and contribute. Masaccio's work at the Brancacci Chapel in Santa Maria del Carmine is a sampling of the more important works studied; their creators and their influence on the art world are listed in the Appendix. These superlative works of artistic expression all existed at the time Michelangelo was a teenager in Florence, so be sure to visit them as part of Michelangelo's trail we are following to see what he saw and studied.

The modern visitor to Florence should make every effort to see as many artworks as possible. From time to time, some of the museums and churches are closed for renovations, so, at any given time, all of the heritage of the masters may not be available to the public. Every museum is not open every day of the week; several are closed on Sunday, Monday or Tuesday. So the visitor must obtain a schedule and carefully plan the time available to catch the key museums on days they are open. If possible, try to avoid the time period from 10 am to 4 pm. Crowds are smaller during the summer months in the early morning and in the later parts of the day after 4 pm.

Michelangelo's best friend Granacci introduced him to Domenico Ghirlandaio, a master painter who was in such demand that he had a *botega* or workshop. Ghirlandaio was the continuation of artistic thought handed down from Cimabue, Giotto and Masaccio with each generation doing better at interpreting nature and improving realism. Granacci himself worked there and assisted the master with his painting work as part of the learning process. Granacci wanted Michelangelo to join him at the workshop so they could learn together. Granacci probably also saw in Michelangelo the seeds of potential talent that could be nurtured by the environment of the workshop. After overcoming the objections of Michelangelo's father, who had a poor opinion of artists because they worked with their hands, Michelangelo was apprenticed to the workshop of Ghirlandaio for three years starting on April 1, 1488 when he was just 13 years old. Most apprentices were older and more mature.

During this time period, Ghirlandaio was working on a major commission, the frescoes of the *Life of the Virgin Mary* and the *Life of St. John the Baptist* in the choir of the church of Santa Maria Novella. This commission was to be a series of frescoes, a medium in which Ghirlandaio was quite expert. It is through the timing of this exposure that Michelangelo learned the basics of fresco painting which were to be the foundations for his later works in the Sistine Chapel. It is believed by some art historians that the young apprentice contributed to a few of the figures in the frescoes. Specifically, some of the figures in the sections regarding the *Presentation* and the *Baptism* are possibly by Michelangelo. In the *Baptism*, the kneeling person and the two people standing behind him are one possibility. In the *Presentation*, the man seated on the steps and the two figures in front of him are also thought to be possible Michelangelo contributions. These figures seem to echo the styles of Masaccio and Giotto of whom Michelangelo was very fond.

Picture 2-1. Piazza Santa Maria Novella with the Church where the young Michelangelo worked on frescoes for Ghirlandaio as an apprentice.

During this apprenticeship period with Ghirlandaio, Michelangelo was also doing some study and sketching on his own. A few of these early drawings survive and are more certainly identified as coming from Michelangelo's hand. These include a drawing after Masaccio's *Tribute Money* in the Brancacci Chapel at Santa Maria del Carmine. Another drawing after Giotto survives from Giotto's frescoes in Santa Croce. A third drawing, after a now lost Masaccio, shows a group of three people standing with the one in the foreground depicted in heavy drapery of his robe. Today these three drawings are in museums in France and Germany. See the list in the appendix

Early Formal Art Training: Giovanni Bertoldo's Medici Garden of Art

While Michelangelo was learning drawing and fresco painting as Ghirlandaio's apprentice in 1488 and 1489, another event in Florence was developing that was to have a major impact on him. The contemporary writer and artist friend/student of Michelangelo, Giorgio Vasari describes the situation in his book, *Lives of the Artists,* written in 1550. Lorenzo Medici was putting together a school for sculptors. Lorenzo already had accumulated a magnificent collection of artwork from his own investing efforts and from his ancestors' collecting efforts. Lorenzo hired Bertoldo to be his curator. Bertoldo had been an assistant in the past to the master sculptor Donatello.

As a follower of the various art movements in Italy, Lorenzo saw the potential decline of sculpturing due to a shortage of current sculpture talent. Painting was going very well with many great artists of the time, but sculpturing was suffering. This was seen as a significant issue because Florence had been the center of outstanding sculptures in the past century. Lorenzo did not want to see the further decline of sculpturing, so he asked the aging Bertoldo to assemble the most promising young sculptors he could find and have them study in his garden under the guidance of Bertoldo. Bertoldo was in the later years of his life at this point and could not work the hammer and chisel as he once had, but he had excellent talent as a craftsman and teacher.

Granacci and Michelangelo both went to the Medici garden to see what opportunities they could uncover. Soon they were both accepted into the Medici school at Lorenzo's garden near San Marco Church on Via Cavour about four blocks north of the Cathedral. The garden is still there but today it is a flower store. Ask to walk through the shop to see the old garden site. (See picture 2-2). This transfer from apprenticeship under Ghirlandaio to school under Bertoldo occurred during the summer of 1489. Michelangelo had studied with Ghirlandaio for only about 15 or 16 months when the switch occurred. But in that time he learned the basics of fresco and tempera painting from Ghirlandaio. Michelangelo had known for some time that his first love was sculpturing, not painting. Now that he had the opportunity to learn sculpturing, he didn't hesitate to seize it. At the age of 14, he was accepted into the school and started training by forming terra cotta figures.

Picture 2-2. The old Medici Garden is behind this wall. Here is where Michelangelo learned to do sculpturing from Bertoldo.

Vasari describes a piece of marble that Michelangelo soon obtained in 1489 at the Medici school in which he carved the head of a faun. He used an antique Roman faun statue in the garden school as a model for his work, but he expanded on it by creating a larger head with more details that showed a wide-open mouth with a lot of teeth. Lorenzo suggested a slight modification with the teeth; his idea was that the age of the Faun would mean that he might be missing a tooth or two. Michelangelo quickly saw the sense of this, chiseled out a tooth and repaired the gum to make it look very natural. Lorenzo was surprised by the ability and skill that the young fourteen-year-old boy showed. This early carving by Michelangelo, probably the first one we have any knowledge of, is now lost.

The marble carving of the head of a faun impressed Lorenzo so much that he invited Michelangelo to live with him and his family at the Medici Palace which was near the garden school that was across the street from San Marco church. The Medici Palace stands today on the corner of Via Cavour and Via de Gori, diagonally across from San Lorenzo Church. It shows on city maps as Palazzo Riccardi.

What an opportunity for the aspiring sculptor! Not only was Michelangelo getting some great training from Bertoldo, but now he was part of the household of the most famous and powerful family in Florence and Tuscany, perhaps even in all of Italy at the time. He was to be raised with the other Medici children almost as one of Lorenzo's own children. These other Medici children would later grow up to be powerful personages in their own right such as cardinals, popes and politicians. All of them were able to learn from the many scholars and humanists that were present in the Medici household at Lorenzo's invitation. Meal-time discussions and discourses in between provided current thinking of some of the greatest minds of the time. These tutors stimulated the young people's thinking on Neo-platonism and classical thought, including Plato, Aristotle, Virgil, Petrarch and Dante. Dante must have left a great impression on Michelangelo; images of Dante's Inferno can be connected with Michelangelo's painting of *The Last Judgement* on the altar wall in the Sistine Chapel several decades later.

As his training in sculpturing steadily progressed under Bertoldo, Michelangelo had the chance to study the many old Roman sculptures that were brought into the garden school through Lorenzo's collecting efforts. These were marble and bronze statues, reliefs and carvings of various types and styles. Soon Michelangelo moved away from working with terra cotta and began working more in marble. Michelangelo seemed especially drawn to the sculptures of the more current works of Pisano, Donatello and Bertoldo. He may even have studied under another sculptor, Benedetto da Maiano, who was popular and well respected at the time. However, he seemed to want a more forceful theme in his carving and he began to study the male nude as a subject for his own work. Male nudes had not been a recent theme of sculpture except for a few cases, like Donatello's bronze *David* from 1430, but the antiquities that he studied used the male nude extensively. Also Michelangelo was impressed by the art of a contemporary painter of struggling nudes by the name of Luca Signorelli.

The 1490's: Early Sculpture Efforts

At this time period, there were two popular themes for artists based on the market demand: religious themes and classical/mythological themes. Inspired by Donatello's two reliefs *Feast of Herod* and *Madonna and Child*, carved between 1425 and 1435, Michelangelo carved his own version of the Madonna in 1491, *Madonna della Scala*. This is now in the Casa Buonarroti in Florence. (Picture 2-3) About the same time period, Michelangelo also worked on a small but dynamic marble relief carving known as *The Battle of the Centaurs and Lapiths*. In this relief, Michelangelo was able to capture the spirit of struggling nudes battling each other in a frenzy of activity and energy. The nude figures seem to emerge from the marble and almost fall out of the marble--the three dimensional effect of the relief is so strong. It is now on display in Casa Buonarroti. (Picture 2-4)

This good time period of study and learning was not to last. On April 8, 1492, Lorenzo Medici died. Michelangelo had been in Lorenzo's household for about two and a half years as his guest. The young sculptor had a great respect for Lorenzo and Lorenzo in turn had a great appreciation for the youngster's developing abilities in marble sculpturing. When Lorenzo's son Piero became head of the household, the same relationship did not continue. Michelangelo left the Medici Palace and returned home to live with his father and four

Picture 2-3. The *Madonna* earliest known surviving sculpture done in 1491 when he was a youth of only 16. Now in Casa Buonarroti in Florence. It measures 22 x 16 inches.

(Alinari/Art Resource, NY)

Picture 2-4. The *Battle of the Centaurs,* a high relief done by Michelangelo in 1492 when he was seventeen years old. He retained possession of this item throughout his life and may have even done a little work on it occasionally. (Alinari/Art Resource, NY)   Approximately 33 x 36 inches.

brothers in their house in Florence on Via Bentacordi. It was about this time that Michelangelo began to study in the evenings at the hospital of Santo Spirito which was connected to the Church of the same name on the other side of the Arno River.   (See picture 2-5). He was not interested in medicine, but he was interested in learning more about human anatomy.

Picture 2-5. This is the facade of the Church of Santo Spirito where Michelangelo studied anatomy at the adjoining hospital.   The muscles and bone structure of the bodies of deceased people were examined before burial since it was not permissible to exhume bodies to do this.   The room where Michelangelo worked is no longer there.

Study of Anatomy at Santo Spirito

Over a period of a few months, Michelangelo dissected and studied several corpses from the hospital before they were buried. This was a clandestine venture that was not favorably looked on by the Catholic Church at the time. Digging up bodies from the grave was expressly forbidden by the church, so examining them before burial eliminated the possibility of excommunication.   The dissection activity to peel back the skin of a cadaver and study the muscles and bones underneath would be a problem for him if the civic and religious authorities discovered what he was doing. But it was a very significant development in the continuing learning curve for Michelangelo. This short but intense period became the foundation for all of his later works in sculpture and painting and helped to set him apart from the others in these fields. It was here he learned about human muscle and bone structures that he used so effectively in depicting the people in his paintings and sculptures with straining and twisting shapes that showed dynamic action and energy. Muscle mass and outlines became a Michelangelo identifier which other artists quickly emulated.

As a token of his appreciation to the Prior of the Santo Spirito monastery and hospital for allowing him to undertake these special studies, Michelangelo carved a wooden crucifixion. It originally hung over the main altar in the church, but then it was moved and its location became unknown. For many years this carving was not recognized as a Michelangelo work until it was rediscovered recently in 1962 on a side altar and restored to its original beauty. The cross itself is not the original cross. There is still some dispute about the creator of the carving of Christ's body on the cross, but enough scholars and researchers believe it was Michelangelo for it to be included in our list of items to see. I saw it at Palazzo Vecchio in a special display that covered the art of the young Michelangelo in November 1999. Normally it is on display in Casa Buonarroti, so look for it there along with the many other items created by Michelangelo. It is referred to as the *Santo Spirito Crucifix*.

Still without a sponsor or commission in 1493, Michelangelo decided to do a marble sculpture on his own to meet his need to carve. He obtained a block of marble and created a *Hercules* in slightly larger than life-size. This was not a relief, but was a full three-dimensional statue in the round, a daring effort by so young a sculptor. It was a preview of finer pieces to come in the not too distant future. *Hercules* was purchased by the Strozzi family for their courtyard as a favor to the young Michelangelo. Michelangelo knew one of the Strozzi boys and one of Michelangelo's brothers worked in the Strozzi family wool business. Later the statue was sold and ended up in France. It was apparently destroyed in 1713.

CHAPTER 3

Michelangelo's First Major Trip: Venice and Bologna

Role of Aldovrandi in Bologna

As Michelangelo was struggling for recognition in the early 1490's and looking for work, the city of Florence was sliding into very unsettled times. Piero Medici was not the leader his father Lorenzo was and he soon found himself in trouble with the political situation. Eventually in the autumn of 1494, Piero was exiled from Florence. Michelangelo saw this turn of events coming so he fled Florence rather than be caught up in the tumultuous political situation. Since he was known to be a friend of the Medici family from Lorenzo's days, he might also be found to be in disfavor with the city council as a Medici supporter. Michelangelo fled his beloved city of Florence and went to Venice in early October of 1494 through Bologna and Ferrara. This was only the first of several times he would leave Florence under negative political situations.

After just a short time in Venice, Michelangelo moved back closer towards home and went to Bologna in November. Here were examples of some artwork of interest to Michelangelo. Jacopo della Quercia was a prominent artist in the 1420's and left many sculptures behind as his legacy. Niccolo dell' Arca was working on statues for the Tomb of St. Dominic when he died in March 1494, just seven months before Michelangelo's arrival.

Michelangelo's presence in Bologna became known to Francesco Aldovrandi, a wealthy nobleman and art patron who had visited Florence on business trips, knew Lorenzo Medici and heard of the young artist. Aldovrandi got in touch with Michelangelo and arranged for him to stay at his home in Bologna while he looked for work. Through Francesco's connections, Michelangelo soon had a commission to complete the statues for the Tomb of St. Dominic that were left undone due to the death of dell' Arca. This was Michelangelo's first true sculpturing commission and was the start of many years of such commissions.

Bologna: The First Commission

St. Dominic's tomb needed three more statues to complete the original concept. One was a *Kneeling Angel* to match the angel that was completed by dell' Arca just before he died. This angel is holding a candle stick and Michelangelo had to design and execute his work to complement the existing angel in size (about 20 inches high) and concept. (See picture 3-1). He did this with no difficulty. The other two pieces to be done were images of two saints, *St. Petronius* and *St. Proclus*. These statues were carved from marble in the round about two feet high. The challenge for Michelangelo was to carve the figures in clothing that looked naturally draped. This was his first known effort to do clothed figures in the round and required a higher level of skill than the reliefs he had done up to this point. Michelangelo worked on these three figures for most of 1495. Scholars make reference to several artists that contributed to Michelangelo's development of these three carvings, including della Quercia, Benedetto da Maiano, Donatello, Verrocchio and some Ferrara painters he had seen on his trip to Venice and back.

The trip to Bologna to see St. Dominic's Church was one of the day trips in which we used the rental car. Even though two of the statues were in Florence at the time for a special display at the Palazzo Vecchio, we decided to go to Bologna anyway to see the Church and the sculpturing work done by other artists. Besides, Michelangelo traveled there. Bologna is the home of a major university and has a history and ambience that is unique from Florence. We also wanted to see the city of Ferrara where Michelangelo visited later in his life with the Duke Alfonso d'Este to study the design of the city's fortifications. More on this later. Bologna is about halfway between Florence and Ferrara on the same highway. Visiting the two cities in one day was feasible with the car. Simply get on Autostrade A-1 outside of Florence and take it north to Bologna. At Bologna connect with Autostrade A-13 north to get to Ferrara. Driving time to Ferrara was about 2½ hours. We stopped in Bologna on the way back to Florence. The highway between Florence and Bologna winds through picturesque valleys and mountains and passes through many tunnels. It approximates the same route that Michelangelo used to get back and forth to Bologna, Ferrara and Venice.

Picture 3-1. The *Kneeling Angel* carved in 1495 for St. Dominic's tomb in Bologna was one of Michelangelo's first commissions as a professional sculptor. It is a candle holder that complements another similar carving on the opposite side of the tomb that was carved by dell'Arca a few years earlier. It is about 20 inches high.

(Alinari/Art Resource, NY)

How Michelangelo obtained his work in Bologna:

There was a law in effect in Bologna to the effect that any foreigner entering Bologna should be stamped on the thumbnail with a seal in red wax. And so, when Michelangelo inadvertently entered without the seal, he was taken to the license office and fined; as he had no way of paying and was standing there in the office, one Messer Gianfrancesco Aldovrandi, a gentleman of Bologna who was one of the Sixteen at that time, noticed him there and, grasping the situation, had him set free, chiefly because he had found out that he was a sculptor. And when he invited him to his house, Michelangelo thanked him ... and went to lodge with him. One day, as he was taking Michelangelo around Bologna, he led him to see the tomb of St. Dominic in the church dedicated to that saint, where two marble figures were missing, which were *St. Petronius* and a *Kneeling Angel* with a candlestick in its hand. He asked Michelangelo if he felt equal to making them and, when he said yes, he arranged for the commission to be given to him and had him paid thirty ducats. The figures are still to be seen in that place.

From *The Life of Michelangelo* by Ascanio Condivi, Pages 18- 19. Translated by Alice Sedgwick Wohl, Edited by Helmut Wohl, Second Edition. The Pennsylvania State University Press, University Park, PA. 1999.

CHAPTER 4

Return to Florence in 1495 and Move to Rome in 1496: the *Pieta* and Starting the Tomb for Pope Julius II

Two Marble Statues and a Ruse

By the end of 1495, Michelangelo had earned the enmity of some other sculptors in Bologna as an outsider who was taking their business from them. He decided to return to Florence now that the political situation had settled down and he felt more secure about living there again.

At the start of 1496 Michelangelo was finishing his 21st year and was looking once more for work. That spring he was able to complete two marble statues. The first was a statue of *Youthful St. John.* It may have been commissioned by a Medici family branch headed by Lorenzo di Pierfrancesco de' Medici who came to know Michelangelo through some consulting work the artist was doing for the City Hall. The statue was done at the time when Savonarola, the Dominican monk, was preaching church and social reforms. At any rate, the statue has been lost. For the past 100 years, some researchers have tried to make the case for its discovery with several similar statues known today, but these efforts have not been accepted by scholars. A possible attribution is the *Young Baptist* in the Bargello Museum in Florence which was originally thought to be by Donatello.

The second statue was a *Sleeping Cupid.* Cupids were a popular subject for sculpturing both in ancient Rome and in contemporary

Florence. This cupid was carved as a suggestion by the same Lorenzo di Pierfrancesco. The suggestion was to make it look like an old cupid from antiquity in terms of carving style and condition. One story relates how the carving was even buried for awhile to make it appear that is was a discovery of a long lost Roman marble. A Roman art dealer, Baldassare del Milanese, who was acquainted with Pierfrancesco and knew of the plot, agreed to take it to Rome and see what he could get for it from some unsuspecting buyer. It was bought by antiquities collector Cardinal Raffaello Riario in 1496 as an antique item. He soon discovered the ruse and became very upset. The cupid was given away and later was sold and traveled to England where it was in the collection of Charles I. Its whereabouts became unknown after 1632.

A Happy Ending to the Plot: Move to Rome

This little episode with the *Sleeping Cupid* had a beneficial ending for Michelangelo. The Cardinal was intrigued with the small carving and its creator even though he had been the victim in the plot. He sent an emissary, Leo Baglioni, to Florence to track down its creator. Michelangelo was contacted and indirectly admitted he was involved. When he learned that Baldassare had been paid much more for the cupid than he had received, Michelangelo became angry, too. With the invitation from the Cardinal to come to Rome, the desire to settle the score with the art dealer Baldassare in Rome and the need to look for work, Michelangelo decided to go to the Eternal City. If nothing else was accomplished, he could at least study the many antiquities that existed in Rome and were still being unearthed. In late June of 1496, Michelangelo moved to Rome and was invited to live at the home of Cardinal Riario. The Cardinal's palace is now the Cancelleria in Rome on Corso Vittorio Emanuele II, a few blocks east of the Vatican. (See picture 4-1).

Michelangelo's trip to Rome probably followed the route south through Poggibonsi and Siena, on to Viterbo and then to Rome. This route was the old Roman Cassian highway that was created to move troops and supplies north from Rome up through the heart of the provinces of Lazio and Tuscany. Today it is a good two-lane highway designated SS-2. We drove it south from Florence as far as Siena and saw the beautiful rolling hills of Tuscany and the Chianti region.

Picture 4-1. The palace of Cardinal Riario in Rome where Michelangelo lived for several months in 1496 and 1497. It is now the Cancelleria office for the Vatican and is located on Corso Vittorio Emanuele II midway between the Vatican and Palazzo Venezia.

Early Work in Rome: *Bacchus* and *Apollo*

Michelangelo found little work in Rome at first. The Cardinal was more interested in collecting true antiquities, not having modern reproductions made for him. Through a friend he knew in Florence, Michelangelo was introduced to a Roman banker named Jacopo Galli. In 1498 Galli was able to take on the role of patron for Michelangelo. His first commission to the young artist was a marble statue called *Bacchus*. This 1498 statue of a standing nude enjoying his drink was a little larger than life-size (80 inches high) and represented the mythological god of wine and revelry. Galli was very pleased with this first work from his protégé. Michelangelo was able to capture the look of drunkenness on the face of the statue and in its posture. Today *Bacchus* is located in the Bargello Museum in Florence. (See picture 4-2).

A second commission by Galli was the *Apollo*. It was a life-size marble statue of a nude that was his perception of the Greek and Roman god of music and poetry as well as medicine and prophecy. The ideal of Apollo's manly youth and beauty were perfect for Michelangelo's interest in human anatomy. The whereabouts of this statue is not known today.

Picture 4-2. The *Bacchus* was sculpted by Michelangelo in Rome in 1498 for a Roman banker, Jacopo Galli.

The *Pieta*

As a result of these two successful sculptures, Galli felt confident enough about Michelangelo's talent to begin recommending him to other wealthy art-patron friends in Rome. One of these connections turned out to be a French cardinal who was an emissary to the Papal Court in Rome. Cardinal Jean Bilheres de Lagraulas had already met Michelangelo and was working out the details of carving a *Pieta* that would be placed in the French Chapel in the old St. Peter's Basilica as a memorial for his service and contributions to the Papal Court.

Before a final agreement was even signed, Michelangelo was authorized to go to Carrara in March and April of 1498 to choose the marble needed for the *Pieta*. Then in August a formal contract was signed with the Cardinal. Galli also signed it as a guarantor of the work being completed and meeting the expectations of the cardinal. There were many paintings of the subject in Italy at the time, but few sculptures had been done so far. France and Germany had some artists sculpturing pietas, but there was nothing of significance attempted in Italy yet. Michelangelo was going to do something nearly original and, as it turned out, revolutionary.

Picture 4-3. The *Pieta* in the first chapel on the right in St. Peter's Basilica. This is one of the greatest marble sculptures of all time. It was completed by Michelangelo in 1499 when he was only 24.

Michelangelo borrowed elements from Leonardo, della Quercia and Verrocchio in creating the most magnificent religious marble statue ever carved. He completed the statue in about two years but the Cardinal did not see it finished; he died in August 1499. To see the statue as it rests today in the first chapel on the right inside the entrance to St. Peter's Basilica is to be moved to a feeling of humbleness and awe. The humbleness comes from seeing the life-like Virgin and Christ and feeling her sorrow as she holds her dead son. The awe comes from realizing what Michelangelo has achieved out of a single block of marble. Emotion and tenderness are both present.

The skill shown in carving and polishing the drapery of the Virgin's clothing, the limp body of her dead son and the spiritual connection between the two figures was revolutionary and has never been surpassed or even matched. Michelangelo was all of 24 years old when he completed his masterpiece. He had managed to combine his interest in carving full-sized clothed figures with his skill in depicting the male torso in various positions and conditions. The skin of Christ appears to be very natural with the veins showing and the relaxed muscles of death beneath. Even the wounds in Christ's hands and feet from the nails seem to be ready to bleed, so realistic is the carving.

CHAPTER 5

Leaving Rome in Anger in 1501:
the *David* in Florence

The *David*

The *Pieta,* even though it was widely acclaimed at the time, did not lead to more work in Rome for the eager sculptor. After a few months of idleness, Michelangelo returned to Florence along the Cassian highway in the spring of 1501. He was probably homesick and he had been informed by friends back in Florence that the City Fathers were considering the commission for the large marble block that had been laying around for a few years in Florence. There was an earlier attempt at carving on it that was started twenty years before and then abandoned. Michelangelo had known of the huge block of marble for several years and he had a few ideas for its possible use. When he heard about the impending decision to give out the commission for the carving of *David,* he had to return to Florence to be considered as a contender for the work. He felt he could do justice to the marble and meet the expectations of the City Council. In addition, he did not want another artist to receive the commission; he felt he was the sculptor for whom the block of marble was meant after two earlier attempts by others failed to result in any progress.

There is another statue similar to the *David* that was carved by Nicola Pisano in 1260. It is *Hercules* in the corner of the pulpit at the Baptistery in Pisa. The shifting of weight to the right foot is nearly identical in both statues. Michelangelo's *David* is much larger at 14 feet high, and it is more forceful in its restrained readiness to do battle against the giant Goliath. Other precedents for the *David* were the bronze statues by Donatello in the 1450's and by Verrocchio in 1475. But both of these representations showed David after he had slain

Goliath; Michelangelo showed David before the encounter and thus depicted a sureness of victory to come from confidence and inner energy. These are the same qualities the Florentine people believed they possessed.

In August 1501, the Board of the Cathedral awarded the commission to Michelangelo when he was 26 years old. The board had heard of his great success with the *Pieta* in Rome and some board members may have even had an opportunity to see it in Rome while there on other business. Piero Soderini, the appointed political leader for Florence, was supportive of Michelangelo from the beginning: it was his influence that helped the award be assigned to the young sculptor.

The original intention for the statue was to place it in front of or on the Cathedral in Florence. When Michelangelo completed the carving in 1504, the powerful image of the marble statue was immediately recognized. It was 16 feet 10 inches high on the base and showed the power and strength on the body and face that was more secular than religious. The Cathedral site was dismissed and a committee of leading citizens and artists of Florence was convened to decide where to place the *David*. After some debate, and with some input from Michelangelo, the site chosen to locate it was in front of the City Hall of Florence. The statue of *David* was seen as a symbol of power and determination to warn all foreign politicians and visitors that Florence was just as determined as David to take on their enemies, no matter how large or powerful. Michelangelo had managed to capture the feelings of civic pride and spirit that existed in Florence in those days when constant threat of battle was present from both outside and inside forces.

Picture 5-1. The *David* in the Accademia in Florence

During the carving of *David*, Michelangelo wanted to keep the progress of the work under wraps from the curious and prying busybodies. He had a special workshop set up in the Opera del Duomo, the maintenance shop of the Cathedral located directly behind the cathedral. Michelangelo worked there for a three-year period and let very few people see the sculpture in progress. His friend Granacci was always allowed to see the carving as it developed. Near the end of the project, Michelangelo permitted Soderini to see the nearly completed statue in the workshop.

A traditional story describes how Soderini observed the statue while he was standing on the floor in the workshop; the statue was on a workstand surrounded by scaffolding and the head of the statue was about 19 feet above him. Michelangelo was on the scaffold near the head when Soderini suggested that the nose of the statue was not quite correct; could Michelangelo please modify the shape of the nose to meet Soderini's preference? Michelangelo hid his frustration with such a suggestion from a person who knew little about such things, especially in the poor lighting and from the angle of view. As he replied he would try to make the change, Michelangelo slyly picked up some marble dust and very small marble pieces from the scaffold in his left hand. He then took chisel and hammer in both hands and proceeded to "chisel" off some more of the statue's nose, slowly releasing the marble dust and particles from the hand holding the chisel tool. From Soderini's distance and viewpoint, it appeared that Michelangelo was doing just as he suggested. Even though the shape of the nose was not affected in the least dimension, Soderini proclaimed the change a great improvement and thanked Michelangelo for accepting his request to modify the nose of David. The civic leader now felt he had truly contributed to the creation of a masterpiece and took great pride in the outcome.

Today the statue of *David* is on display in the Accademia Belle Arti Museum on Via Ricasoli, three blocks north of the Cathedral, where it is protected from the weather and other harm. It was moved to the Accademia in 1873 and a reproduction now stands in its place in front of City Hall (Palazzo Vecchio). In 1527, when the original statue was in front of City Hall, the left arm was damaged during a dispute in one of the meeting rooms above it when a chair was tossed out of a window of the building and hit the statue on the way to the ground. The damage was repaired so today it is barely noticeable.

Other Activities in Florence: 1501 to 1505 and The *Tondi*

While he was working on the statue of *David,* Michelangelo was engaged on other projects at the same time. (Some researchers place them in the period 1505 and 1506). Two of these were round marble reliefs called roundels or *tondi.* They are identified by the names of the families for whom they were carved. They show that Michelangelo was continuing to be fascinated with the subject of the Madonna and Child. The marble *Taddei Madonna* portrays an off-center Madonna holding the Child Jesus as he leans away from his cousin St. John the Baptist who has a fluttering bird in his hands. Jesus is about two years old as depicted in this roundel which is 46 inches in diameter. Today the *Taddei Madonna* is at the Royal Academy in London.

The second roundel is called the *Pitti Madonna.* It centers the Madonna and Child in the relief which is 33 inches in diameter. Both roundels show chisel marks from the various carving techniques that Michelangelo used. Very little if any polishing was done on these two marble roundels so it is easy to see how the sculptor worked the marble with his chisels and created an image that reflected the wishes of the families who commissioned them. The reasons why they are not polished to a smooth finish like the *David* are not clear today. This may have been due to being very busy with so much work, or in the case of the *Pitti Madonna,* Michelangelo may have been called to

Rome before the work was completed and the Pitti family accepted it as it was. Today the *Pitti Madonna* is in the Bargello Museum in Florence.

Picture 5-2. The *Pitti Madonna* in the Bargello Mus. in Florence

Other work that was undertaken by Michelangelo in this time frame includes a painted *tondo*. This piece was painted for the Doni family so it is called the *Doni Madonna* or *Doni Tondo*. It is made of resin and tempra painted on a round wood piece 47 inches in diameter. As the only known easel painting widely attributed to Michelangelo, it was criticized immediately as not up to his normal standards. Even in the later period of the late 1800's, some art critics and historians were writing negative comments about the work.

Later critics saw it as a precursor to images created by Michelangelo in the Sistine Chapel a few years afterwards and praised it for its muscular style and strong forms in unusual twisting positions. The sculpturing style of painting seems to make the three central figures stand out from the background in a three-dimensional effect. It has very bright crisp colors and the Madonna can be seen as similar to the Delphic Sibyl figure in the Sistine Chapel ceiling. Now the *tondo* is in the Uffizi Gallery in Florence in the next block south of the Palazzo Vecchio.

A Project in Siena: The Piccolomini Altar

A fourth Madonna of this period is the marble statue called *The Bruges Madonna*. The original purpose of this beautiful statue is not known for certainty today. Some scholars believe it was intended for the Piccolomini tomb in the cathedral in Siena. Francesco Piccolomini in Siena was a cardinal who saw his memorial tomb as needing the attentions of a master like Michelangelo. In 1501 he commissioned several marble statues from Michelangelo for the tomb in the Siena Cathedral where he expected to be buried. Other sculptors and artists were already at work on the tomb project since 1481. Michelangelo received a contract to produce 15 statues for the tomb in a three-year period and was not to undertake any other work in that time period so the project would be finished on time. In 1501, he traveled to Siena, probably along the Cassian Highway, to get the measurements needed

for the dimensions of the statutes as they would be placed in various niches on the tomb.

As we know from above, Michelangelo did in fact take on other projects in the same time period which was common to do because of the uncertain events that could interrupt a commission at any time. Artists usually had several projects going at once to maintain a steady flow of work. Michelangelo did work on four known marble statues for the tomb. These are *St. Francis, Pope Pius I, St. Paul* and *St. Peter.* He must have also started the Madonna, too. But he was so busy in Florence on the other projects that he basically stopped work on the Piccolomini commission.

Picture 5-3. The Cathedral in Siena, site of the Piccolomini altar. Repair scaffolding covers the left portal.

In September 1503, Piccolomini became Pope Pius III. The election of the new Pope motivated Michelangelo to get back to work on the project. Unfortunately, the Pope died suddenly a few weeks later in October 1503 after only 28 days as Pope. He was buried at the Vatican in Rome, not in Siena as he had planned. The tomb was switched to an altar by the surviving Piccolomini family. Michelangelo again slowed work at that point on the project; he still had a binding contract to honor for the estate which he turned over, along with the marble supplies, to another sculptor, Baccio da Montelupo. Apparently the Madonna and Child we now know as *The Bruges Madonna* was executed for this commission by Michelangelo and later sold to the wealthy Mouscron family in Belgium in 1506 when a decision was made not to use it in the altar. The statue is now in the Notre Dame Cathedral in Bruges, Belgium. According to scholars, the Madonna has elements of Donatello and Jacopo della Quercia in the style Michelangelo chose to portray Mary's face and drapery.

The trip to Siena to see the Cathedral and the Piccolomini altar is a full-day trip. It is not that far, but there is so much to see in Siena in

Picture 5-4. This is the corner of the *Fonte Gaia*, in Piazza del Campo, Siena, created by Jacopo di Pietro, known as della Quercia. This rectangular basin was completed in 1419. Copies were created in 1858 and the originals were moved into a near by museum for safety.

addition to the Cathedral. Travel to Siena can be by bus, car or train. To get there, we took the 90-minute drive south from Florence along the ancient Cassian Highway (named after the Roman Consul who had it built, Cassio), SS-2 and engaged a tour guide (Tours by Roberto) in Siena to assist us. We walked the wonderful old town section and saw the plaza (Piazza del Campo) in front of the town hall (Palazzo Publico) where the fountain (Fonte Gaia) by Jacopo della Quercia was of interest to Michelangelo for its strong relief sculpturing. (See picture 5-4). The hospital museum (Santa Maria della Scala) is also a major point of interest for visitors with many historical artifacts and works of art regarding the history of Siena.

The hospital contains the original Quercia fountain parts which have deteriorated over time while they were in the fountain outside in the plaza; reproductions are in the fountain in the plaza now. Our return to Florence from Siena was on the Superstrade, a non-toll expressway; it took only 45 minutes, but it was not as scenic as the route down from Florence on SS-2.

The Council Chamber Fresco in Florence: *The Battle Of Cascina* in Sala dei Cinquecento

While all this activity was going on with Michelangelo, he was involved in yet another project. It seems that the City Council of Florence wished to have the large main wall of the council chamber painted with frescoes. This wall was huge at 200 feet long and 40 feet high. After some consideration, the decision was made to give the left half of the wall to Leonardo da Vinci and the right half to Michelangelo. Neither artist was too pleased with the situation, but they each jumped right into the project. Michelangelo choose as his subject the *Battle of Cascina*. After some study of soldiers in the field, Michelangelo prepared a large cartoon as part of the normal

Picture 5-5. Palazzo Vecchio, the old city hall in Florence, site of Sala dei Cinquecento

process of painting a fresco. The cartoon was sketched on paper and would be used to transfer the drawing to the wall through a series of small holes in the paper that followed the outline of the drawing. The artist would mount the paper on the wall and put a colored chalk dust on the holes which would leave the outline on the wall after the paper was removed. Much time was used to prepare the cartoon. It was a magnificent drawing that attracted many artists to see it. They proclaimed it a masterpiece in itself and used it as a study tool for their own developing talent.

Unfortunately, the painting never was completed. Michelangelo was called away to Rome by the demanding new Pontiff, Pope Julius II. The cartoon remained in Florence, but it was in such demand that it became worn and damaged through folding and rolling it up. Eventually it was cut down into smaller pieces and now is lost.

However, we know what it looked like through the efforts of a contemporary artist who made a copy of the central part of it. Aristotle da Sangallo's copy made in 1542 is now in a private collection in England.

Cathedral Figures in Florence

As if he wasn't already busy enough, concurrent to this project was
a commission from the Cathedral in Florence for Michelangelo to
carve 12 marble figures of saints at the rate of one a year. The marble
blocks were delivered from Carrara in December 1504 and
Michelangelo proceeded to work on them. The first one started was
St. Matthew. It was never completed and the others were not started.
The reason is that the summons from Rome by the Pope was too
strong to ignore. Today, the *St. Matthew* statue is in The Accademia
in Florence. It is believed by some historians that Michelangelo may
have done more work on the statue in April to November 1506 when
he returned from Rome for awhile. As it was left unfinished, the body
of St. Matthew seems to be emerging from the marble, almost as if
coming out of a foggy night. The result is a unique piece of artwork
that has an unusual appeal to the viewer. At nearly nine feet high, it
makes a dramatic piece of sculpture.

CHAPTER 6

Second Trip to Rome in 1505:
The Sistine Chapel

Pope Julius Calls

In March 1505, Pope Julius II summoned Michelangelo to Rome. The news brought great joy, expectation and pride to the Buonarroti family. Lodovico, long critical of Michelangelo's choice of a career as a sculptor, had been persuaded by his son's success with the *Pieta* and the *David* that perhaps Michelangelo was in the right line of work after all. This new recognition from the Pope seemed to restore and confirm the prestige for the family.

When Michelangelo left to go to Rome, he left several projects in Tuscany unfinished. These were the 12 saints for the Cathedral, the battle scene on the wall of the Council Chambers, and the Piccolomini altar in Siena. A fourth project, an unfinished painting on wood, now identified as *The Manchester Madonna*, is also believed by some art historians to be a Michelangelo effort in this time period. However, if it was done by Michelangelo at all, it was also probably worked on by another artist as well. The painting is now housed in London, but it was on temporary display in Florence in November 1999 where I saw it when the research for this book was being done.

Pope Julius was in the process of rebuilding the Basilica of St. Peter. The original structure was about 1100 years old and was a maintenance nightmare. Emperor Constantine had commissioned the construction of the venerable church in 315 AD and the centuries afterwards had taken their toll on the building. It was now nearly impossible to make the dilapidated basilica meet the needs of the Papacy without spending huge sums of money. Pope Julius decided to tear down the old basilica and replace the church with a new larger edifice more in tune with the ideas of the Renaissance. Bramante was the architect engaged by the Pope to be the chief architect and builder. He was the preeminent architect of the period and had built several other churches in Italy. His ego and Michelangelo's ego would soon clash.

The Tomb of Pope Julius II and Quarries at Carrara

For his first assignment to Michelangelo, the Pope wanted him to design and build a tomb for his mortal remains that would someday require burial. When Michelangelo perceived that the Pope would be interested in a grand plan for a huge tomb, he let his creative juices flow. Several proposals were sketched out by Michelangelo in a short time for review by the Pope. The final design that was finally approved in 1505 was a magnificent design for the marble tomb unlike any other known, which is just what Pope Julius felt was appropriate for the recognition of his contributions to the Church and to Rome. The base was to be 23 x 36 feet and it was to be 40 feet high. Forty statues were to be carved and mounted on various platforms and niches. Michelangelo committed to finishing the tomb in five years. He would later regret letting his ambition get ahead of his judgement. The project interfered with his piece of mind for nearly forty years until a smaller version was completed. But for now, the young sculptor was so elated he could not wait to get started.

In late April of 1505, just a few weeks after arriving in Rome, Michelangelo had the Pope's agreement on the design of the tomb and the commission was finalized. Michelangelo went to Carrara to supervise the quarrying of the tons of marble needed for the tomb. He spent eight months in Carrara selecting the raw marble while it was still bound in the mountain side. He climbed and surveyed and chiseled and cut large blocks from the choicest part of the quarry. He assisted in moving the large blocks down the mountain side to the waiting wagons that would move the marble to the coast for transport by ship to the seaport near Rome. Then they were loaded onto wagons at the seaport and moved to the workshop in Rome where they could begin to be shaped by Michelangelo for the tomb and carved for the statues planned to decorate the tomb of Pope Julius II.

Picture 6-1. The quarries at Carrara north of Pisa where Michelangelo found the marble that best met his needs for his sculpturing work.

A visit to Carrara to see the marble quarry is an exciting trip that will take you into the countryside again. It is best done from Florence with a rental car. From Florence, take Autostrade A-11 west towards Pisa. At Lucca take the north branch towards Viareggio. Go past A-12 to SS-1 and turn north towards Genoa. Soon you will cross under A-12 and enter the quarry district of Pietrasanta. You will pass marble holding yards and sales yards filled with all sizes and shapes of the white stone waiting for shipment or buyers. Continue north toward Seravezza, another quarry town just a few miles away. Proceed on through the town of Massa and arrive at Carrara about 2½ hours after leaving Florence. You will go past dozens of marble staging yards and workshops along the way from Pietrasanta to

Carrara. The air seems to be filled with very fine white marble dust from the nearby quarries and from the marble staging yards.   In Carrara, follow the quarry signs through downtown and east up into the foothills.   Watch out for the large quarry trucks carrying marble down to the staging yards along the road back to Carrara.

After approximately three miles, you will be winding through the hills where the marble mines are located. From across the valley you can see the great scars in the earth where huge quantities of marble have been removed over the centuries. With a little patience, you will soon see and hear the great blocks of marble tumbling down from the heights of the mountain to the staging pick-up point below. (See picture 6-1).   By using binoculars you can see the people and equipment moving about on the marble shelves created by past efforts. Not much has changed since Michelangelo did the same work in 1505. In staging yards along the road up to the quarry area, you will see marble blocks nearly as large as a room in a house. (See picture 6-2).

Picture 6-2. Examples   of   quarried marble ready to be moved from mountainside staging yards to the seaport docks.

After viewing the quarry activity, return to town and proceed to the seaport for Carrara. There you will see the arriving marble trucks lined up for unloading with the typical seaport cranes found around the world. Marble blocks are transferred from the trucks to the ships waiting in the harbor. We saw a dozen ships being loaded or waiting to be loaded. Each piece of marble was marked with symbols to identify its source and its new owner. The port activity is about the same as when Michelangelo was there except the cranes are larger and run by electricity instead of manpower, pulleys and winches. We took the whole day to drive to the quarries, see the activity, have lunch, poke around in some shops and drive home on the same route we took to get there. (See picture 6-3 for the seaport activity).

Picture 6-3. Shipping activity at the docks in Carrara where the huge marble pieces are loaded onto ships for transport to various processing studios around the world. The marble blocks today are similar to the size of the blocks used in Renaissance times.

Michelangelo made several trips to Carrara and the other marble quarry towns over the following years for various projects. This eight-month trip in 1505 for the Julius II tomb was the longest stay he endured. In later trips for other projects, he was told to avoid the Carrara marble quarries since Carrara was outside the Florentine sphere of influence and thus not under the control of the Pope. For some projects, he was restricted to marble from Seravezza and

Pietrasanta, even though he tried to convince the Pope that the Carrara marble was superior in quality and purity.

When Michelangelo returned to Rome late December 1505, he was really charged up and ready to start work on the marble parts of the tomb for the Pope. However, there were some major delays in transporting the material to Rome and weeks went by before it arrived. In the meantime, the Pope was shifting his interest and funds to other projects. These included the rebuilding of the Basilica of St. Peter's and the restoration of the Papal territories at Bologna. Both projects were major consumers of time and money and the result was that Michelangelo's tomb project was ignored. The impatient sculptor was not reimbursed for the purchase of the marble or for the costs of transportation to move it to Rome without some aggressive follow up on his part.

As the time stretched into months with no support from the Pope to proceed on the tomb, Michelangelo became increasingly frustrated with the situation. Finally, after several fruitless attempts in one week to meet with the Pope, Michelangelo left Rome very quickly and went to Florence on the old Via Cassian Highway. On the way there, he passed through Poggibonsi, which is just north of Siena, and rested there overnight. This was Florentine territory so he was safe from the wrath of the Pope who became very angry with the sudden departure of his sculptor. The Pope's messengers who caught up to the artist in Poggibonsi were unable to convince Michelangelo to return to Rome.

Since Michelangelo was between projects when he arrived in Florence in April 1506, he just puttered around on some of the partially completed projects that he left unfinished in 1505. He probably worked on *St. Matthew* for the Cathedral and on the *Battle of Cascina*. The Pope summoned Michelangelo back to Rome several times during the next few months, but the stubborn sculptor refused to return. This really began to upset the city fathers in Florence who were being threatened by the Pope for apparent lack of support in getting Michelangelo motivated to return to Rome.

Bologna Again: A Bronze Statue of Pope Julius II

By November of 1507, the Pope had retaken Bologna and had become increasingly upset with Michelangelo; so had his Florentine patrons. Finally the artist capitulated and agreed to meet the Pope in Bologna. Michelangelo traveled to Bologna and met the Pope at San Petronio and Palazzo de' Sedici. The scene was rather tense as Michelangelo walked through the group of people visiting the Pope and made his apology. However, he was forgiven and told he was once again in good graces.

The easy victory the Pope had in regaining Bologna was probably of some help in creating the forgiving attitude on the part of the Pope. In fact, Michelangelo received another commission from the Pope, one he did not particularly want. However, he was in no position to refuse it after a mild attempt to decline it. This commission was for a bronze statue ten feet high of a seated Pope Julius II that was to be placed in San Petronio Church in a niche over the main doorway. Michelangelo was not experienced in bronze casting so he summoned some help from bronze workers in Florence to assist him. He still was forced to cast the statue twice when the first attempt was only partially successful. By July of 1507, he had a good casting; now all he had to do was the finishing work of scraping and polishing. This tedious work was finally completed in March of 1508. The bronze piece was installed in the cathedral niche as planned. Unfortunately, the casting was destroyed in December 1511 when the citizens of Bologna rioted in rebellion to the Pope's appointed administrator. The statue was melted down to use the bronze for a new canon.

In March, 1508, Michelangelo is back in Florence working on *St. Matthew*. During this trip he purchased the house on Via Ghibellina. It is now the Casa Buonarroti, a museum that contains many of the artist's works not housed in other museums. Michelangelo never lived in this house, but his nephew Lionardo did and later descendants willed it to the city of Florence. This is well worth the admission fee charged today. It is at the corner of Via Ghibellina and Via M. Buonarroti just two blocks north of Santa Croce Church. Walk north on Via de Pepi from the Santa Croce Plaza in front of the church to Via Ghibellina and turn right for one block.

The Frescoes of the Sistine Chapel Ceiling

In April, Pope Julius II summoned Michelangelo to Rome again. This time he wanted Michelangelo to paint the ceiling of the Sistine Chapel. At first, Michelangelo tried to decline the commission since painting was not his first choice of assignments. But, once again, the Pope prevailed and Michelangelo commenced work in May of 1508. The Pope was convinced that Michelangelo's talent would produce a

magnificent painting on the ceiling of the new chapel that was recently finished a few years earlier.

Picture 6-4. The imposing fortress-like exterior of the Sistine Chapel. Here Michelangelo labored for 4 years to create the world's greatest ceiling fresco for Pope Julius II.

Michelangelo labored for 4½ years to complete the ceiling of the Sistine Chapel. When he unveiled it in August of 1511, with the lunettes still not painted, people were amazed at what he had accomplished. Even the Pope was impressed. During the last year and a half of work, the Pope kept pestering Michelangelo as to when he would finish the painting. Michelangelo's reply was always "when it is done". The special scaffolding Michelangelo had constructed to enable him to work at the height of the ceiling blocked the view of progress from down below at the floor level. But the Pope would climb the scaffolding to get an up-close look and check on progress. When the scaffolding was removed and the entire ceiling could be seen, it was an awesome sight even in the critical view of the Pope.

Some scaffolding was set up again and Michelangelo took another year to complete the lunettes. The final unveiling of the ceiling was on All Saints Day, November 1, 1512. The themes of the Bible and the use of brilliant colors and foreshortening to compensate for the angle of view from 80 feet below were marvels of composition and execution. Today one is overcome with admiration for the result and for the painter who accomplished it even though it was not his favorite type of work. A visit to the Sistine Chapel is a must for any visitor to Rome. Enter it through the Vatican Museum's entrance and follow the crowds and signs through the museum to the Chapel. Find a seat on one of the benches along the side walls so you can more easily see the ceiling while sitting down. It also helps to take a small pair of binoculars with you to more closely study the ceiling. Don't forget to look at the altar wall to see the later painting by Michelangelo named *The Last Judgement.* We'll discuss it more later.

During the time Michelangelo was working on the ceiling of the Sistine chapel, he set up a permanent workshop in Marcel de' Corvi, a small street near the Capitoline Hill near Trajan's Column. He worked here until his death. Unfortunately, the workshop and surrounding areas were destroyed in the late 1800's when the monument for Victor Emanuelle II was built. One can still walk in the area of Piazza Venezia, get a little flavor of the neighborhood, and imagine Michelangelo working in the shadow of the Roman Forum just a block away, or making his way west on one of several streets to the Vatican to continue his work on the Chapel. We walked the route through Campo Fiori and the narrow streets that today have many interesting stores and shops of various craftsmen. Many of the present antique buildings along Via Giulia and Via del Pellegrino were there in the early 1500's. This is a pleasant walk through a true Renaissance street not clogged with cars and mopeds. The variety of shops and restaurants will cause you to make slow progress as you head haltingly towards the Vatican or the Piazza Venezia, depending on which direction you are walking.

CHAPTER 7

Another Effort on the Tomb for Pope Julius II

Moses and the *Captives (Slaves)*

During the period from 1513 to 1516, Michelangelo worked on some of the statues for the tomb of the Pope. The *Moses* was the most significant of the statues that were agreed upon in the earlier contract. This is a larger-than-life size marble carving of a seated prophet Moses; it is 100 inches high even in the seated position. Scholars differ as to when he started the carving; the range runs from 1506 to 1519. Regardless of the timing, it is a superlative example of the skill Michelangelo had for carving marble and capturing the forcefulness of expression and the power of the person. Today the statue rests in front of the final and much smaller Julius tomb in San Pietro in

Vincoli. This old church is located on the hill a few blocks north of the Coliseum just off Via Giovanni Lanza. Also to be seen while there are the original chains that bound St. Peter before his death; hence the source of the name of the church which dates back to 439 AD.

Picture 7-1. This depiction of *Moses* by Michelangelo for the tomb of Pope Julius II created much discussion regarding its power of expression and fine detail. The contemporary biographer Vasari wrote in 1568 that there was nothing to rival it in either ancient or modern sculpture.

Two other marble statues for the tomb were also worked on in this time period. These are the *Two Slaves (or Captives)*. Of the six statues started with a slave or captive theme by Michelangelo, these two are the most complete. Today they are in the Louvre Museum in Paris. The other four *Slaves* are in the Accademia in Florence, the same place that the *David* is on display. The latter four were carved in the time period 1530 to 1533 and are barely half-finished. Yet they convey the unmistakable power that was to define the tomb of the Pope.

The *Risen Christ*

During this same time period in the later teens of 1500, Michelangelo also carved a marble statue of the *Risen Christ*. This large carving of 6 feet 10 inches high was commissioned by three wealthy citizens of Rome. Michelangelo had to carve it twice; the first attempt resulted in the discovery of a black flaw in the marble that appeared in the face of the statue. He stopped work on the flawed marble and started over from the beginning on a new block of marble.

Picture 7-2. *Risen Christ* in the church of Santa Maria sopra Minerva

The second attempt was done in Florence where he had returned to work. He sent the statue to Rome not quite finished and charged his assistant Pietro Urbano to complete it. Urbano's finishing touches in 1520-21 were not of the same quality that Michelangelo would have achieved, and there were some negative comments about this at the time. However, the statue was accepted by the commissioners and put into place in March 1521. The final product is still on display in the church across the square from the Pantheon. The church is Santa Maria sopra Minerva, so named because it was built over the Temple of Minerva in the 8th century. The original unfinished and flawed carving is now lost. It was last seen in 1556.

About the time all this was going on in 1514 to 1516, Michelangelo designed the facade of the Leo X Chapel in Castel Sant' Angelo in Rome near the Vatican. This was a marble design and may be the first known completed work in architecture by Michelangelo. It has been "restored" so the two upper rectangular windows have replaced the two original circular windows. This is more in line with an early facade drawing attributed to Giambattista de Sangallo who was a contemporary of Michelangelo. Older pictures in some books show

the original design by Michelangelo that was in place before the restoration. (See picture 7-3).

Picture 7-3. The Chapel Facade in Castel Sant' Angelo, one of Michelangelo's earliest known architectural efforts prepared for Pope Leo X.

Picture 7-4. This is the Castel Sant' Angelo on the Tiber River where the popes had secure apartments for refuge when invaders came to Rome. It is the remodeled tomb of Hadrian that was originally built in the 2nd century. The Chapel of Pope Leo with its facade designed by Michelangelo is located in this castle.

The Start of the San Lorenzo Facade and the Medici Projects in Florence

After May, 1516, Michelangelo spent most of his time in Florence. Pope Leo X asked him to work on several projects for the Medici family in their hometown. In late 1516, Michelangelo made several more trips to Carrara to select marble for the Chapel of San Lorenzo. He was designing the chapel and the facade for the church, too. His workshop was established on Via San Zanobi. In December, 1516, he presented drawings of the facade of San Lorenzo to Pope Leo X for approval. In early, 1517, a scale model of the facade was being made of wood so the Medici family could get a better appreciation of what was to be accomplished. The church was completed in the 1470's, but the facade was never started; it was left unfinished and, in fact, is still

rough and unfinished today. (See picture 7-5). The wooden scale model of the proposed new facade was completed in the summer of 1517 and is available for viewing today in Casa Buonarroti.

Picture 7-5. The unfinished facade of San Lorenzo Church in Florence. Michelangelo designed a new facade for the Medici family church that was accepted, but the construction was never funded. The facade appears today as it did in the Renaissance period.

In spite of Michelangelo's acceptable design and his enthusiasm for the project, three years were spent in trying to get the needed quality of marble. The Pope became impatient, and the contract for the facade was eventually canceled in March, 1520. Part of the problem centered around the fact that Michelangelo preferred the marble from Carrara but the Papal territories had recently acquired the quarries at Pietrasanta and Seravezza, just south of Carrara along the coast of the Ligurian Sea west of Florence. The Pope restricted marble sources for his family's church to these two latter quarries. This made the people in Carrara angry enough they decided to make life difficult for Michelangelo by interfering with boat transport of the marble from the two Papal properties.

In March and April, 1519, Michelangelo visited Genoa and Pisa to try to arrange for other boatmen to help with the transport of the marbles. Besides the stress of the situation, Michelangelo nearly wore himself out constructing new roads to move the marble blocks from the Pietrasanta and Seravezza quarries to the seaside shipping ports for loading into the boats for transport to Florence up the Arno River.

During this time, however, Michelangelo was able to find a good marble block to replace the defective material he originally used for the *Risen Christ* described previously.

Other work was given to Michelangelo by the Medici. Perhaps, since they knew what a great talent he had in marble sculpture and fresco painting, they suspected his latent genius would also blossom in architecture if given the opportunity. A smaller project of window design was therefore given to the artist. The windows he created are on the ground floor of the Medici Palace in Florence. Some

Picture 7-6. This is one of four similar windows in the Medici Palace believed to be designed by Michelangelo about 1520. This palace is called Palazzo Riccardi today and is located at the corner of Via Cavour and Via de Gori, just a block from the Cathedral.

scholars believe he created only the two windows on the main facade next to the entrance on Via Cavour.   Others think he was also responsible for the two windows on the side street, Via de Gori. These four windows were added when the Medici family decided to enclose the loggia or ground-floor porch and gain more private living space in the palace. The one-inch iron grill work was added for security later. Today the windows show the massive strength of design of Michelangelo and confirm that the Medici's were great judges of unrecognized talent. (See picture 7-6).

While all this was going on, Michelangelo was working on designs and marble selection for some of the other Medici projects in Florence. These were the *Medici Library,* the *Medici Tombs,* and *the New Sacristy* or *Chapel.* In December of 1520, he completed a model for the Chapel and in April, 1521, he went to Carrara to get more marble material. This project was proceeding well and he was allowed to complete it. During the middle years of the 1520's Michelangelo spent most of his time in Florence working on these significant projects. See chapter nine for more details about these projects. He made occasional trips to Rome to visit with the Pope during this period of time, but fled hurriedly in May, 1527, when the Spanish army sacked Rome. The Pope remained safely in Rome in the fortress of Castel Sant' Angelo. The plague finally drove out the Spanish after seven months of pillaging.

How Michelangelo achieved the San Lorenzo jobs:

Pope Julius died (February 1513) and on the creation
of Pope Leo the work of the Julius tomb was laid
aside, for this new Pontiff, no less enterprising and
splendid in his undertakings than Julius, was
anxious to leave in his native city of Florence, of
which he was the first Pope, some great memorial of
himself, and of that divine artist who was his fellow
citizen. He therefore commissioned Michelangelo to
execute the facade of the Church of San Lorenzo in
Florence, which had been built by the House of
Medici. Much talk arose on the subject of the works
to be executed in Florence. The undertaking like that
of the facade of San Lorenzo ought certainly to have
been divided among many persons. Regarding the
architecture, several artists repaired to Rome,
applying to the Pope for the direction thereof. . . . But
Michelangelo determined to prepare the model
himself, and not to accept any guide, or permit any
superior in the matter of the architecture. This
refusal of all aid was nevertheless the occasion of
such delays that neither by himself nor by others was
the work put into operation.

From *Lives of Seventy of the Most Eminent Painters, Sculptors
and Architects* by Giorgio Vasari. Edited and annotated by E. H.
and E. W. Blashfield and A. A. Hopkins, Volume IV, pages 108-110.
Charles Scribner's Sons, New York, 1896.

CHAPTER 8

Winds of Political Change Endanger Michelangelo in Florence

The *Victory* and Politics

After his departure from Rome in the spring of 1527, there was plenty for Michelangelo to do in Florence. He had work on various existing projects, including the *Tomb of Julius II*, the *New Sacristy* at San Lorenzo and the *Medici Library*. Michelangelo took on some additional projects one of which was the *Victory*. We aren't sure today where this marble statue was intended to be placed; some think it was for the *Tomb of Julius*, others for the facade of San Lorenzo before the contract was canceled. The majority of scholars put it in the group of statues made for the Tomb. It is believed the piece was done in the 1527 to 1530 period which makes it too late for the facade effort. The marble statue makes an impressive piece as a twisting *Victory* stands over the vanquished, depicted as an old man.

Picture 8-1 . This is the *Victory* as it appears in the Palazzo Vecchio in Florence (City Hall). It is in the huge meeting room where Leonardo da Vinci and the young Michelangelo were to each do a fresco on the wall behind the statue. Michelangelo's fresco was to be *The Battle of Cascina.*

Apparently, Michelangelo did not complete this effort; it was finished by an assistant. Even so, the polishing is not complete and only one eye has the pupil carved into it--the right eye. Today, the *Victory* can be seen in the Palazzo Vecchio in Florence.

Picture 8-2. The *Victory* is the statue in the center. This is the meeting room, the great hall Sala del Cinquecento, which is the room Leonardo and Michelangelo were to do their competing frescoes in 1506. Each fresco would have been about 100 feet wide and 40 feet high if completed.

About this same time, Michelangelo received another commission for a statue that would be complimentary to his earlier *David*. The commission was originally given to another artist in 1525, but the political situation changed and Michelangelo was given the commission in August 1528. This was the *Samson Fighting the Philistines*, also called *Hercules and Cacus*. Efforts got as far as making a clay model for the statue, but no work in marble is known today. We know about its design from a bronze casting made of the clay model by a contemporary artist, Pierino da Vinci. The bronze is in the Frick collection in New York.

Fortifications in Florence

Political issues were heating up in Florence in the late 1520's. Florentines had forced out the city rulers, the Medici. Pope Clement VII, a Medici, was threatening to take control of Florence for the Papal States. Michelangelo was engaged to help with the designs of the fortifications of the city. His area of focus was on the hill of San Miniato, directly south of the city across the River Arno. This hill was in a strategic spot that needed special protection to keep it out of enemy hands lest the enemy mount cannons on it to shower the city down below. By walking up the hill through the city streets today, the visitor can see the remains of old fortifications and protective walls and gates. These probably were built after Michelangelo's time, but are very worth the visit to get a flavor of the defensive challenge and

 because of the great views of the city from the height of the hill.(See 8-3). Michelangelo's earthen ramparts have long disappeared.

Picture 8-3. The hills on the south side of the city near San Miniato where Michelangelo worked on fortifications to protect the city from invaders. His earthen works are now gone.

In April, 1529, Michelangelo was elected Governor and Procurator General of all the fortification of Florence. In June, he traveled to Pisa and Livorno to examine their defensive systems for any possible applications in Florence. In July, Michelangelo visited Ferrara to see their fortifications. He stayed with his friend from the past, the Duke Alfonso I d'Este, at his castle which is still standing today in the center of Ferrara on the Piazza della Republica. His wife was the infamous Lucretia Borgia. Begun in 1385, it is a huge, great-looking castle building with a moat around it just like you would imagine a Renaissance castle to look. (See Picture 8-4). Many of the nearby defensive walls erected by the Duke are still visible today mixed in among the buildings and parkways a few blocks from the castle. (Michelin's 1998 guide book has a map that shows the old walls for easy location on page 112).

Picture 8-4. The castle of Duke Alfonzo in Ferrara where Michelangelo stayed while studying the nearby fortifications in 1529. Ideas obtained here and elsewhere on the different fortifications were applied back in Florence by Michelangelo.

Try to do the Ferrara trip combined with the trip to Bologna in one day as described earlier; Ferrara is just 29 miles north of Bologna on the Autostrada A13 and S64. You can park near the castle for a short time in the Plaza if you let the local police on foot in the area know you won't be there long. Other pay-parking facilities are nearby within an easy walk. We parked in the Plaza long enough (about 20 minutes) to view the castle from outside and walk two blocks to see the Duomo built in the 12th century. It is a great example of Romanesque and Gothic styles and must have left an impression on Michelangelo when he visited there in 1529.

When he visited the Duke Alfonso I d'Este in Ferrara, he was asked by the Duke to do a painting. This was to fulfill an earlier agreement made in 1512 when the two men became friends after meeting in Rome at the Sistine Chapel. The Duke had asked Michelangelo to do a painting for him sometime in the future. Now the agreed upon subject was *Leda and the Swan*. The painting was completed by Michelangelo in late 1530, but the Duke did not ever obtain it. When the Duke's emissary came to Florence to obtain the painting, he made some disparaging remarks about the painting. Michelangelo became angry and sent the emissary back to Ferrara empty handed. In the following year, the painting was given as a gift to Michelangelo's assistant Antonio Mini to help him with dowry expenses for his two sisters and for expenses for a trip to France. The original painting is now lost, but copies by other contemporary artists help us see how it looked. One can see a marked similarity of this painting to the reclining figure of *Night* that Michelangelo was carving for the Medici Chapel tombs. Also, there is a drawing of the head of *Leda* by Michelangelo that still survives. It is in Casa Buonarroti in Florence.

Flight to Venice and Return to a Hide-out in Florence

When Michelangelo returned to Florence full of new ideas for the city's defenses, he was not welcomed. The leaders of the new republic felt he was not to be trusted since he was so involved in the design of the fortifications of the city. When he uncovered possible treason within the defensive organization, he saw the sensitivity of the situation and fled to Venice in September where he spent only a few weeks. However, while there, Michelangelo submitted a design for the new Rialto Bridge to cross the Grand Canal. The existing bridge was a dilapidated structure that was a hazard to cross. His design was not accepted and the drawing of Michelangelo's proposal is not known today.

By November 23, 1529, Michelangelo was back in Florence and allowed to continue his work on the fortifications; his ideas were valued over his questionable allegiance. Since he tended to be apolitical, it was felt his allegiance was to the city and not to a faction, so his input was considered useful. His status as outlaw was rescinded. This tense truce was soon exploded when the treason suspected earlier by Michelangelo came to reality. Treaties with the Pope were agreed upon to keep the city from being invaded and sacked. In September, 1530, Florence was controlled by a Spanish commander who allowed reprisals to be taken in violation of the treaty. Michelangelo had to go into hiding to avoid being caught up in the turmoil again.

With the help of a trusted friend, Michelangelo found a hiding place in a small room under the altar of the Medici Chapel. He lived there about eight weeks and managed to avoid being detected. While there, he did some sketches on the walls which are still visible today. He apparently obtained some charcoal and occupied himself with several sketches which relate to the sculpture work he had been doing for the tombs to go into the Medici Chapel. Visitation to the room under the altar is restricted but is possible with the help of a guide to get the special permissions needed. We had the authorization with our guide to enter the well-guarded stairway that went down to the room through a small trapdoor on the left side of the altar. For about fifteen minutes, three of us were allowed to view the sketches done by Michelangelo during this self-imposed confinement. Pictures without flash were allowed and therefore taken. (See picture 8-5 a and b).

This hiding room was not commonly known as a room of Michelangelo's drawings until 1975 when it was discovered by accident. Apparently it was used as a dark, unlit storage room for many years and later the trapdoor was covered up with storage items. The sketches were not noticed until recently when a clean-up program was undertaken. The sketches show the genius of Michelangelo and are a special highlight of a trip to Florence. Inquire about special art guides in Florence at the Visitor's Center Tourist office who can assist

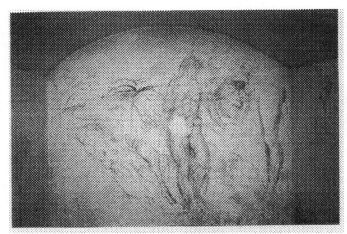

Pictures 8-5 a and b. These show two of several charcoal drawings one by Michelangelo in the secret storage room below the altar in the Medici Chapel in Florence. He hid out in this room for about eight weeks to avoid likely political persecution.

with the arrangements to see the sketches in the storeroom under the altar. You can also find our guide, Ugo Primadei, who was a very helpful and knowledgeable guide in Florence. He took excellent care of us for two days and was a great source of information about Michelangelo and his activities in Florence.

Apollo

As a result of his being reestablished in the good graces of the city politicians, Michelangelo carved a marble statue of *Apollo* or *David* in 1530-31. This statue is 57 inches high in the round. It is fully carved except for the details at the base, but it is not polished. It is thought by some scholars to have been carved as a gift to ease the tensions with Baccio Valori, the temporary Florentine governor, after the restoration of the Medici family control. The statue is in the Bargello National Museum in Florence for viewing today. (See 8-6).

Picture 8-6. This is the *Apollo* sculptured about 1530 as a political gift from Michelangelo. It is now in the Bargello Museum in Florence.

CHAPTER 9

The Medici Projects at San Lorenzo Church in Florence

The Medici Chapel

Now let us turn our attention again to the Medici Chapel, its tombs and the Medici Library, where Michelangelo poured in a lot of his energies during the thirteen years from 1521 to 1534. There is a remarkable amount of Michelangelo's work in these Medici projects in Florence.

We already know that the project for the facade of San Lorenzo was canceled earlier, but these other projects continued to be developed and are clear evidence of the talent of Michelangelo in architectural design and marble sculpturing.

The Medici Chapel at the Church of San Lorenzo, often referred to as the *New Sacristy,* was commissioned by Pope Leo X who was the current leading member of the Medici family in the early 1520's. This Chapel was to complement the earlier chapel on the other side of the main church which was created by Brunelleschi in 1421-28. The basic design of the *New Sacristy* developed by Michelangelo was limited so it would agree with the earlier chapel by Brunelleschi and it was to be built on the foundation started by Brunelleschi 100 years earlier. Michelangelo's new chapel was completed in 1524; the purpose of it was to be the tomb for four of the Medici family members. Only two were finally entombed there.

Pope Leo X died in December 1521 and a new pope was elected who was not a Medici. He died after about two years and another Medici, a cousin to Leo X, was elected pope who took the name Clement VII. This was helpful to Michelangelo who now was given more complete responsibility for all of the Medici projects in Florence to the exclusion of other artists. These other artists had been circling like vultures hoping for some of the work to come their way.

Inside the Medici Chapel, there are seven major marble sculptures to honor the two Medici tombs which were worked on by Michelangelo and are viewable today. Four of these marble sculptures are referred to as the "Four Phases of the Day". On the tomb of Duke Lorenzo are *Dusk* and *Dawn* in their uninhibited poses while across the chapel the tomb of Duke Giuliano has the figures of *Night* and *Day* reclining in similar fashion. These four reclining figures are not completely finished; *Dusk* and *Day* still need carving work around the heads, the hands and the feet. All of the statues need polishing. These four statues were carved between 1524 and 1534. (See pictures 9-1 & 2).

Picture 9-1 and 2. Tomb of Giuliano de' Medici (L) and Tomb of Lorenzo de' Medici (R) in the Medici Chapel at San Lorenzo Church in Florence. Michelangelo carved all six of the statues over a ten year time period.

Above each tomb in the niche is a marble statue of the seated Duke, though there is no likeness intended; these are idealized representations. One represents the Active Life (Giuliano) and the other represents the Contemplative Life (Lorenzo). Each statue is very large; seated they are nearly six feet high. Michelangelo had the help of some of his assistants in carving several of the minor details in order to accomplish all the work involved. The posture of the two figures of the Dukes are similar to the poses of some of the figures in the fresco paintings in the ceiling of the Sistine chapel. These two statues were also carved between 1524 and 1534.

On the wall between the two tombs opposite the altar are three more statues. In the center is the marble statue of the *Medici Madonna*. This massive sculpture of a seated Madonna and Child, with her legs crossed, in the round is 7 ½ feet high and is not finished either. The positions of the two figures recall the Madonna and Child in a turned position in Michelangelo's first sculpture of this subject--the *Madonna of the Stairs*, carved in relief in the 1490's.

Picture 9-3. The *Medici Madonna* as it appears in the Medici Chapel in Florence. Completed about 1534. The two side statues of St. Cosmas and St. Damian are not by Michelangelo.

In the *Medici Madonna*, the right arm of the Madonna seems awkward in its backward twist as though a flaw in the marble or a mistake by the carver forced a change in execution. The polishing work is not complete as close-up pictures reveal the fine chisel marks left by Michelangelo. The lower third of the statue is less and less complete the lower you look. The pedestal upon which the Madonna is seated is only roughed out and the feet of the Madonna and the Child are not finished. The web of marble is still present under the foot of the Madonna and the back of the statue is still very rough. This statue was carved in the 1524 to 1534 time period.

The two statues beside the *Medici Madonna* were not done by Michelangelo; other sculptors executed them based on Michelangelo's designs. They portray St. Cosmas and St. Damian. One of the altar candelabra, the one on the left, was carved by Silvio Cosini based on a design by Michelangelo.

The effect of the entire room is an awesome impression of nobility and grandeur. As visitors enter the chapel and feel the presence of Michelangelo in the seven major marble carvings with the very large tombs of the Dukes, they can be overwhelmed with so much powerful art in such a small space. The tombs, the Dukes in the niches and the Madonna are all set up in high levels in the walls so visitors must look up at them which adds to the feeling of awe. The two Dukes and the celebrant of mass at the altar all face towards the Madonna as Michelangelo deliberately designed the arrangement. We visited in November at a time when not many people were in the chapel, perhaps 15 to 20. With a more crowded room as is possible in the summer tourist season, the overpowering feeling may be much reduced. This chapel became the school for aspiring artists to study and learn the marble sculpturing techniques of the master.

The Medici Library

The other effort by Michelangelo in this San Lorenzo complex is the Library which was being designed and constructed at the same time as the Chapel.   Pope Clement VII commissioned the design to Michelangelo in 1524 shortly after he was elected Pope. Michelangelo did the first designs immediately and included the vestibule with the cascading steps, the library room itself with the floor, ceiling, walls and library benches all created by the artist. Construction of the room and steps stretched out over several decades until 1559.   Other contemporary artists did the actual work from Michelangelo's designs.   These included Vasari and Ammanati on the stairs, Battista del Tasso and Antonio Carota for the ceiling, Tribolo on the floor and the carved benches by Battista del Cinque and Ciapino. Since space was at a premium even then, Michelangelo was given permission to build the library over the convent of the church. The exterior of the library can be seen from the cloister courtyard which was designed by Brunelleschi. (See picture 9-4).

Picture 9-4. The cloister courtyard at San Lorenzo which shows the Medici Library as the top two floors over the original structure on the right.

While visiting this complex of San Lorenzo, be sure to see the interior of the church, too. It has many beautiful appointments designed by Brunelleschi and Donatello, earlier Renaissance masters. In addition, there is a sacrarium designed by Michelangelo to hold sacred relics of saints collected by Lorenzo de' Medici. Michelangelo designed the *Tribune of the Relics* in 1526 and the construction was completed about 1533. It is located over the doors of the main entrance of the church inside the front wall and faces the main altar. Michelangelo also designed the *Coat of Arms* of Clement VII in the shape of the skull of a horse which is under the little balcony over the front doors. (See Picture 9-5). This was one of the few pictures that were bright enough inside the church to capture the details adequately. Most church interiors were poorly lit for picture taking.

Picture 9-5. This is the inside of San Lorenzo Church in Florence looking at the inside of the front entry. Michelangelo designed the section behind the the railing where relics of saints are kept. It is called the *Tribune of the Relics* and was completed in 1533.

CHAPTER 10

Renewed Efforts on the Tomb
for Pope Julius II

A Revised Contract for a Smaller Pope Julius Tomb

In April, 1532, Michelangelo made a trip to Rome to meet with the heirs of Pope Julius II to renegotiate the contract for the tomb for the third revision. In this round of discussions, the design was cut down to include only six statues, three of which were to be carved by Michelangelo and three others by contemporary artists. It had originally started with forty statues, but after four designs, it was now a lot less opulent and more practical. This was quite a concession for both the artist and the descendants of the Pope. Everyone was interested in seeing the tomb completed; after all, it was initially started in 1505, twenty-seven years earlier. Michelangelo was so frustrated with this project that he wrote later in a letter he would have been better off in his life if he had started his career making matches instead of carving marble statues.

Even though he was still working on the Medici Chapel and the seven tomb carvings in Florence, he also was carving the marble *Captives* for the Pope Julius tomb. There are two sets of *Captives* (also called *Prisoners*) and a total of six known carvings. The first two statues were actually completed in 1516 and are referred to as *The Heroic Captive* and *The Dying Captive*. Unfortunately, they became excess when left out of later tomb designs that reduced the size and scope of the tomb. After 1546, they ended up in France and became property of the state during the Revolution in 1794 and today are in the Louvre in Paris.

The Four *Captives* and *Rachel* and *Leah*

The second set of *Captives* were also intended for the Julius tomb and are known today as *Youthful Captive, Atlas, Bearded Captive* and *Awakening Captive*. They are marble carvings in the round and range in height from 8½ feet to 9 feet 2 inches. None of these captives are as finished as the first two, but, as a result, they enable us to better understand the carving technique and process used by Michelangelo as he worked the marble by carving from front to back. Michelangelo worked on them in the 1520's and 1530's. These four statues never made it to the Julius tomb either, but instead were placed in the Boboli Gardens in Florence after Michelangelo's death. Then in 1908, the four sculptures were moved to the Accademia in Florence where they remain today.

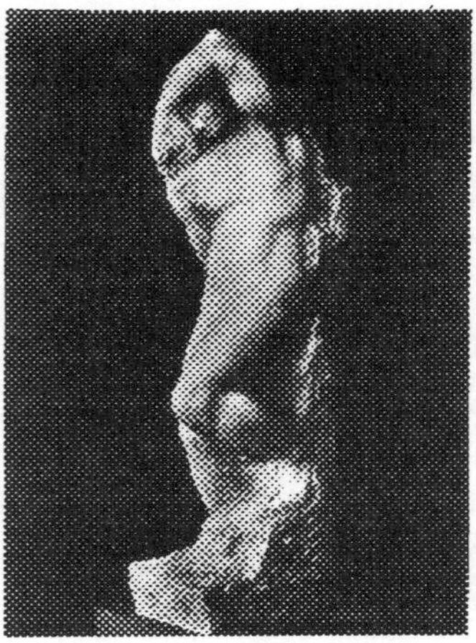

Picture 10-1. *Youthful Captive* in the Accademia, Florence. (Alinari/Art Resource, NY)

We have already described the statue of *Moses* that Michelangelo carved for the tomb and completed in 1516 except perhaps for some polishing final touches. This statue did make it through the many design changes that affected the tomb and it is the central focus of the tomb today as it appears in S. Pietro in Vincoli. By itself it would be a suitable monument for any but the most vain personality. Two other statues are beside the *Moses* and were conceived as a result of the design changes. Since the *Captives* were no longer needed for the tomb now that they were too large for the scaled down design, Michelangelo suggested two new ideas, in another tomb contract in 1542, which were made in scale small enough to be used in the remaining niches of the tomb. These two are *Rachel* and *Leah*, alternatively known as *Contemplative Life* and *Active Life*. Where have we heard that before? (The Medici Chapel)

These two late additions to the Julius tomb, *Rachel* and *Leah*, were 6 feet 7 inches and 6 feet 10 inches high. Together with the *Moses* statue, they were installed in the niches of the tomb in 1545 in S. Pietro in Vincoli in Rome where they remain today. These two female figures, probably inspired by Dante's *Purgatorio*, were the last ones by Michelangelo that he finished with polished details.

Picture 10-2. The tomb of Pope Julius II in its final design version in the church of St. Peter in Chains. The *Moses* is the center dominating statue that is recognized as the most powerful statue of Moses ever carved. The two statues on the lower level beside Moses are *Rachel* and *Leah*, also sculptured by Michelangelo for the tomb. This is the project that consumed 40 years of Michelangelo's time from 1505 to 1545.

Evidence of the Julius II Tomb pressure on Michelangelo:

"If I'm allowed a reasonable time, I'll do the figures myself. I'll always go on working for Pope Clement with such powers as I have, which are slight, as I am an old man—with this proviso, that the taunts, to which I am being subjected, cease, because they very much upset me and have prevented me from doing the work I want to do for several months now. For one cannot work at one thing with the hands and at another with the head, particularly in the case with marble. Here it is said they are meant to spur me on, but I assure you they are poor spurs which drive one back. I haven't drawn my salary for a year now, and I am struggling against poverty. I have to face most of the worries alone, and there are so many of them that they keep me more occupied than my work."

From a letter by Michelangelo, 24 October 1525, to Giovan Francesco Fattucci, a chaplain from the Florence Cathedral, who became the agent for Michelangelo in the negotiations regarding the unfinished tomb of Pope Julius II.

From *The Life of Michelangelo* by Ascanio Condivi as quoted in *Michelangelo, His Life, Works and Times* by Linda Murray, Thames and Hudson, New York, 1984.

CHAPTER 11

New Commissions in Rome Starting in 1534:
Last Judgement, Conversion of St. Paul, Crucifixion of St. Peter

The *Last Judgement* for the Altar Wall In the Sistine Chapel

Throughout the 1520's and early 1530's Michelangelo was traveling back and forth between Florence and Rome and the marble quarries. Many of these trips were of short duration and had the purpose of meeting with the Pope or Medici family Cardinals for various contract negotiations. He had workshops in both cities, but the one in Rome was primarily a storage room during this period. His active marble carving was being done in Florence. However, in September, 1534, Michelangelo made his last trip to Rome; he did not return to Florence for the rest of his life, which lasted another thirty years.

Michelangelo was nearly 60 years old in 1534 and the rigors of his work and the stress of travel were starting to wear him down. Travel by horseback one way between Rome and Florence took several days at that time. Also, some new assignments in Rome kept him quite busy there for the next few years. Unfortunately, two days after he arrived, Pope Clement VII died. The Pope had been working with Michelangelo on a design for a painting to depict the Resurrection of Christ for the altar wall of the Sistine Chapel.

In late 1534, the new Pope, Pope Paul III, commissioned Michelangelo to paint the fresco above the altar in the Sistine Chapel. However, the subject was changed from the *Resurrection* to the *Last*

Judgement.   Michelangelo worked on the design and cartoons for about 18 months before starting the actual work on the wall in the summer of 1536. To absorb the new painting and keep it in good condition, a new brick and plaster wall was constructed over the altar which eliminated a window and sloped the wall slightly outward as it rose to the top near the ceiling. The fresco painting was completed in 5 1/4 years and turned out to be a very controversial masterpiece.

Counter-reformation ideas were less tolerant of the nude figures Michelangelo had portrayed in this huge wall painting over the altar which measures 48 feet by 44 feet.   It was unveiled on October 31, 1541, and motivated the Pope to fall to his knees when he saw it in its entirety.   Criticism of the original painting as a "bathing establishment" and charges of irreverence finally resulted in the decision to paint over some of the offending areas. This was less harsh than some suggestions to destroy the entire fresco. The over-painting began in 1559 from the direction of Pope Paul IV. Fortunately, the first artist to be assigned the over-painting of the fresco was Daniele da Volterra who happened to be a good friend and student of Michelangelo's. Another artist may not have had the same respect for the master's work as da Volterra did.

The Council of Trent in late 1563 finally addressed the controversy and decreed that the representation of certain unsuitable subjects in churches was forbidden.   Further over-paintings occurred in 1572, 1625, 1712, and 1762. Michelangelo had the last word in a way: he painted his critics into the fresco and portrayed one of them as the figure of Minos (the Devil) and the other as Bartholomew holding the skin of the slain martyr (the face in the skin has similarities to Michelangelo himself).   As a visitor to the Sistine Chapel, be sure to look at the altar wall to see this significant work by Michelangelo; don't spend all of your time looking at the ceiling. In addition, there are frescoes by other great masters on the side walls that predate the ceiling and the altar wall.

During this time period, about 1537, Michelangelo met Vittoria Colonna, a younger woman who was a widow and a modifying influence in the religious reformation that was moving through Italy. She had a great influence on Michelangelo's art and poetry; for her he created several beautiful drawings of the Crucifixion which still exist today. Most of them have been moved to museums outside Italy in subsequent ownership changes since they were very portable compared to the large and heavy marble statues and much more subject to sale by various past owners.

Brutus

About 1539-40, Michelangelo was asked by a friend from Florence to carve a *Brutus* for Cardinal Nicolo Ridolfi. This friend, Donato Giannotti was a Florentine exile living in Rome. He was a historian who had been the Secretary of War after Machiavelli in the last Florentine republican government. They worked together during the siege of Florence in 1529 and had common interests in the defense of San Miniato where Michelangelo assisted with the fortifications. In 1539, Giannotti commissioned Michelangelo to do a bust of *Brutus* for the Cardinal as a commemorative piece for the past Republic. Michelangelo's patriotism and fondness for Florence led him to agree to do the bust. However, before it was completed, he was reminded of the criminal nature of Brutus's deed and he left the bust unfinished. In his mind, Michelangelo seems to have equated Brutus with Judas, a traitor to authority. Some historians suggest that the bust was a reminder for him of the assassination in church of Lorenzo's brother, Giuliano de' Medici, in the political turmoil of 1478 in Florence.

The unfinished piece was given to Tiberio Calcagni, a contemporary sculptor of lesser ability who worked with Michelangelo. Calcagni did the drapery of the bust and some flat chisel work on the face, but even he did not finish the bust with polishing. The chisel marks are still very clear on the face of the piece when viewed close up. Michelangelo did not use the flat chisel during this period; it was a tool he used earlier in his work but by now he had changed to a finer tool. Today the bust of *Brutus* is in Florence in the National Museum of the Bargello. (See picture 11-1).

Picture 11-1. *Brutus* as depicted by Michelangelo about 1542. Now in the Bargello National Museum in Florence.

The Vatican Pauline Chapel Frescoes: 1542 to 1550

In the Pope's private chapel, called the Pauline Chapel, Michelangelo was asked to paint two frescoes. While the chapel is not generally open to the public, the two frescoes are well represented with photographs in art books. These frescoes were the last ones painted by Michelangelo. They took several years to complete due to the time diverted to finish the tomb for Pope Julius II and the fact that Michelangelo was ill intermittently during these years. They are *The Conversion of St. Paul* and *The Crucifixion of St. Peter*. Each fresco is about the same size as the other--approximately 21 feet by 22 feet. They were completed by Michelangelo when he was 75 years old in 1550. The first one of them finished, the *Conversion of St. Paul,* was damaged by a fire in 1545 and restored by Michelangelo. Other restorations were done as late as 1933.

CHAPTER 12

Architectural Projects in Rome

The Campidoglio Projects

About a year after his arrival in Rome in 1534, Michelangelo was appointed the Chief Painter, Architect and Sculptor for the Vatican Palace. This did not include responsibility for St. Peter's Basilica, but, nevertheless, it was quite an honor and showed how determined the Pope was to sink his hooks into Michelangelo so he would not return to the distractions of other projects in Florence.

In 1538, Michelangelo was also starting to get more involved in architectural projects in Rome. About this time, Pope Paul III decided that the Campidoglio needed some attention; after all, it was the civic center of Rome but it was in no condition to even show to visiting dignitaries. The first step was to move the statue of Marcus Aurelius from its then current location in front of the Lateran Church to the Campidoglio. A new pedestal was to be designed by Michelangelo for the statue to be mounted on. This was accomplished in 1538 and the pedestal is still under the statue as set by Michelangelo in the center of the piazza. (See picture 12-1).

In the same time period, Michelangelo was asked to design the entire piazza and improve the existing buildings. This he did with his great design of the piazza itself that used geometric shapes made of contrasting colored stones. He also designed the steps for the Senatorial Palace (see picture 12-2) and the facade of the Conservatori Palace in 1538-1539. The Senatorial steps were started in 1544. The Conservatori Palace was already in place and Michelangelo designed the front of the building; it was built later in 1568 according to his design as an early form of urban renewal.

Picture 12-1. This is the statue of Marcus Aurelius mounted on the pedestal designed by Michelangelo for the center of the city hall square or Campidoglio. The design of the patterns in the pavement stones is the original design as created by Michelangelo.

Picture 12-2. A view of the Senatorial Palace behind the Marcus Aurelius statue. Michelangelo designed the steps of the Palace in 1538-39. More of the patterns in the pavement can be seen as designed by the master.

Across the piazza from the Conservatori Palace is the Capitoline Museum which was also designed by Michelangelo a little later but not completed until about 1665 after Michelangelo's death. It has the same design for the facade as the Conservatori Palace. Because of his death in 1564, many of the projects in the Campidoglio were altered in their design to varying degrees before being completed by subsequent designers. However, the paving design we see today with its geometric swirling patterns adheres to the original design thanks to the restorative work done in 1940. The ramped walkway up to the top of the Campidoglio hill from the street below, Via de Teatro di Marcello, is also of Michelangelo's design according to some historians.

The Palazzo Farnese

Picture 12-3. The third floor facade of the Farnese Palace in Rome was designed by Michelangelo who used the original designs of the windows created by another architect. Michelangelo added to the height of the space over the windows.

Another major project that attracted Michelangelo was the bidding to finish the Palazzo Farnese. This building had been started in 1517 but had only reached up to the third story without the facade being completed. Bidding for the design of the third story facade was opened to obtain new ideas for its completion when the original

architect died in 1546. Michelangelo's design was selected for the
second story center window over the main entrance and for the
cornice design at the roof line. (See picture 12-4). The original
architect's designs for the other third floor exterior windows were
accepted by Michelangelo, but he made the third story facade higher
than the original plans had specified.

Picture 12-4. This is the 2nd floor
window over the main entrance to the
Farnese Palace in Rome that was
designed by Michelangelo in 1546.

Inside the courtyard, the frieze of swags and masks was a
Michelangelo contribution. The third story courtyard windows were
a major design of Michelangelo's. Note especially the decorative
features of the ram's head with braided garland within the floating
crescent above each window and the heads of lions on both sides of
each window. Notice, too, how the pilasters between the windows
are used to add the appearance of strength to the third floor facade.
There is no attempt to tie in the heavier looking third floor pilasters to
the more delicate first and second floor columns of Doric and Ionic
style except for their vertical alignment with each other. The cornice
at the top of the third story is also unique with its masks and dentil
blocks repeated every few inches with cookie-cutter precision.

Picture 12-5. This shows some of the frieze design created by Michelangelo at the top of the Farnese Palace in Rome. It is similar to the frieze around the top of the inside court- yard.

The Belvedere Niche at the Vatican

At the Vatican, Pope Julius III wanted to improve the Belvedere Niche in one of the courtyards. The original lower story and curving stairs were designed by Bramante in 1503. He was an arch rival of Michelangelo's and had been commissioned by Pope Julius II to design and build the new Basilica of St. Peter in the early 1500's. Now the current Pope, Pope Julius III, wanted new stairs for the Belvedere Niche that looked like the stairs at the Campidoglio which Michelangelo had just completed. Michelangelo obliged the Pope and designed the double flight of opposing stairs that can be seen today when you exit the Vatican Museums into the courtyard. Alterations to the stairs since Michelangelo's time have added the balustrade and the fountain with the mask. Also added were the peacocks and the huge pine cone, but the stairs are still to Michelangelo's original design. He also influenced the design of the niche to make it higher, but Piero Ligorio completed the work in 1562 with some modifications. (See picture 12-6).

Picture 12-6. The Belvedere Niche on the Vatican grounds had the designs of the steps and the dome influenced by Michelangelo.

The Porta Pia Gateway in Rome

Another architectural project that Michelangelo was given is the Porta Pia. It was part of the new gate and street improvement program that the Pope had initiated. It was commissioned by Pope Pius IV in 1561. Michelangelo designed the gateway for the ancient Aurelian Wall as we see it today except for the central tower which was added later after Michelangelo's death, collapsed in the 1580's, and then replaced in 1853. He had the help of several assistants in the stone work and the sculpturing; Jacomo del Duca did the coat-of-arms of the Pope based on the master's design. Porta Pia was completed after Michelangelo's death. This gateway is on the east side of Rome where Via 20 Settembre and Corso d'Italia intersect, a few blocks east of Villa Borghese. It was completely covered with scaffolding for cleaning when I attempted to view it in November 1999. One of Michelangelo's drawings done about 1561 for Porta Pia now is in Casa Buonarroti in Florence.

Michelangelo's Last Two Design Efforts

The Sforza Chapel in Santa Maria Maggiore was one of the last architectural efforts by Michelangelo. He worked on it in 1560. After his death, his design was carried out by his assistant Tiberio Calcagni and, later, by Giacomo Della Porta. It is considered a very advanced design and is quite complex for its time period. Santa Maria Maggiore is located three blocks south of the train station and three blocks northwest of Piazza Victorio Emanuele, so it is within an easy walk of Santa Maria degli Angeli described in the next paragraph. Be careful not to confuse this Piazza with the Monument to Victorio Emanuele II at the Piazza Venezia.

The last architectural effort by Michelangelo was the design for the conversion of the Baths of Diocletian into the Church of Santa Maria degli Angeli. He started this design work in 1563, just the year before he died. Later architects, especially Liugi Vanvitelli, modified Michelangelo's concepts in the eighteenth century so his original design is no longer visible. The new church made out of the old ruins of the Baths is beautiful and well worth the visit, especially when you consider that Michelangelo had a hand in the early rebuilding and conversion to a church. Santa Maria degli Angeli is located at the Piazza della Republica, just a few blocks northwest of the train station, Statione Termini. There is a convenient subway stop at the Piazza della Republica. Visit Santa Maria degli Angeli on the same trip to see Porta Pia; they are within a few blocks of each other. (See picture 12-7).

Picture 12-7. The ancient Baths of Diocletian were converted in the Church of Santa Maria degli Angeli. Michelangelo contributed to the design work just a year before his death. Even today, the church doesn't look like much other than a Roman ruin from the outside, but inside it is a magnificent place of worship.

Picture 12-8. One of the interior doorways of Santa Maria degli Angeli believed to have been designed by Michelangelo during his last year of work in 1563.

CHAPTER 13

Michelangelo's Design for St. Peter's Basilica at the Vatican

A New Appointment by the Pope

On January 1, 1547, Pope Paul III appointed Michelangelo the superintendent of works of St. Peter's Basilica. This made him a successor to the original architect, Bramante, who had started the construction in the early 1500's to replace the old Basilica built by Constantine early in the fourth century. Michelangelo was the fifth architect to have this great responsibility for the design and construction of the venerable church. He decided to use the original concept that began with Bramante forty years ago and was subsequently deviated from by the intervening architects, Raphael and the two Sangallos, Giuliano and Antonio.

When Michelangelo took responsibility for the completion of the Basilica, the main floor plan had not been completed, but the Sangallo design, which elongated the church, was discarded in favor of the original Bramante design. Construction work on the Sangallo design was stopped and much of it was torn down. Many observers were critical of this change and the wasted effort and money. Permission for this change was given and supported by Pope Paul III at the time and reaffirmed by subsequent popes. In fact, Michelangelo was given complete freedom to make whatever changes he wanted. Michelangelo's final design was supported by papal decree stating that no further changes were to occur and any other architects that might become involved must use these latest plans. This was a key issue because the construction of the Basilica was a not a continuous activity; money shortages and political intrigues frequently interrupted the work and stretched out its completion date by several decades. The main portion of the present Basilica that exists today was completed to Michelangelo's design.

Design Changes and a Wooden Model

Picture 13-1. A view of the dome of St. Peter's Basilica from the Vatican Gardens with early morning sunlight. This design is the crowning work for the master architect and came so late in his life he did not live to see it completed.

Knowing that the construction of the remaining unfinished dome portion of the Basilica would take longer than he would probably live, Michelangelo had a wooden model of the dome prepared to serve as a guide for those who would complete the effort. This model was constructed from 1558 to 1561. Today it can be seen in the St. Peter's Museum in the Vatican. The idea worked because the finished dome is very close to the wooden model.

During the design phase, Michelangelo considered several different concepts for the dome. These included the dome of the Pantheon which was the old Roman shrine on the piazza in front of Santa Maria sopra Minerva which we visited earlier. He even arranged to get the measurements and design of the dome created by Brunelleschi for the Cathedral in Florence. Michelangelo's final design was incorporated into the wooden model. The dome of the Basilica was completed by a series of architects after Michelangelo's death in 1564. Vignola, Giacomo della Porta and Domenico Fontana all worked on the dome and it was not completed until fourteen years later.

Picture 13-2. A close-up view of the dome from the roof of the Basilica. This finished masterpiece of design closely followed Michelangelo's concept after his death because a detailed wooden scale model was constructed to ensure later architects did not deviate from his design.

When the Basilica was finally completed in 1578, dome and all, it was a magnificent building that demonstrated the architectural genius of Michelangelo. The dome was his architectural masterpiece and could be viewed from any angle around the Basilica. However, later additions to the Basilica changed this and destroyed the view angles that Michelangelo had considered while creating his design. In the period from 1607 to 1623, the Basilica design was again modified by an extension of the nave, but the completed work up to 1607 was not altered. The nave was extended by Carlo Maderno with a baroque architectural style that was becoming popular at the time.   While present day visitors exclaim over the impression of great grandeur the Basilica now possesses, the addition of the nave in front of the Basilica obscures the view of the dome from the piazza.   The best close-up view of the dome today is from the Vatican Gardens on the hillside behind the Basilica. (See picture 13-1). Be sure to schedule a walking tour of the gardens so you can see the beauty of the dome and how well it is designed to merge with the basilica below it.

To really understand the immensity of the project for the time it was built, one should take the journey to the top of the dome. An elevator can be taken up to the Basilica's roof level at the bottom of the dome, but a winding and narrow staircase will need to be conquered to reach the high point at the base of the lantern. The entry for the climb is to the right side of the Basilica towards the back of the alleyway. One can look down on the transept and nave of the Basilica from the inside mezzanine at the base of the dome and begin to realize what a monumental achievement the basilica is, not only in design, but in construction, too. This structure was assembled over 400 years ago with methods and tools much more primitive than those in use today.

Picture 13-3. As one looks down on St. Peter's Square from the dome of the Basilica, the roof of the later extension of the nave by Maderno can be seen in the lower section. The 284 columns by Bernini in the two curving colonnades, completed in 1667, link the city of Rome to the Vatican.

CHAPTER 14

The Final Sculpture Works: the Pietas

The *Florentine Pieta:* 1548 to 1556

While Michelangelo was engaged in the many other painted and architectural projects described above, he never stopped working on his first love, marble sculpture. During the years from 1448 to 1555, he was working on another *Pieta.* This would be his second great work of art in marble using the theme of the dead Christ just after removal from the cross in the arms of his mother. Michelangelo's biographer, Georgio Vasari describes this piece in his 1550 book on the *Lives of the Artists,* so we know it was started a couple of years

before the book was published. Later, Vasari, while writing his second edition of the book, mentions the same piece as nearly finished in 1556. This sculpture is thought to have been intended for Michelangelo's tomb; the artist was in his early seventies when he began the work on it and he realized the end of his life was approaching. (See pic. 14-1).

Picture 14-1. The *Florentine Pieta.* (Alinari/Art Resource, NY)

Today the *Florentine Pieta* is located in the Opera del Duomo, the workshop behind the Cathedral of Florence. It consists of four figures with Christ as the central figure supported by Nicodemus, Mary and Mary Magdalene.

The face of Nicodemus is thought by many to be a self-portrait of Michelangelo. The artist worked on this marble piece in the evenings after his other work was done for the day as a form of relaxation from his fresco painting work. According to Vasari, his biographer, Michelangelo even rigged up a hat with a candle wedged into it so he could see what he was doing after darkness fell. The other contemporary biographer, Ascanio Condivi remarks on the superlative skill that Michelangelo still shows at 75 to create such a laborious piece in marble with the four figures each distinct with the folds of their clothing separated from the others. It stands an imposing 7 feet 8 inches high.

Unfortunately, like all of the later sculptures, this piece is not finished. Near the end of the carving, a flaw in the marble was discovered and Michelangelo struck the carving with his hammer in frustration. He broke the left leg of Christ which explains why there is only one leg showing in the statue. The left arm of Christ was also broken but the pieces were saved and replaced as we now see them. Many observers don't even notice the missing left leg with all the focus being directed to the three figures holding the dead body of Christ to prevent it from falling to the ground.

Michelangelo gave the unfinished and now damaged *Pieta* to Francesco Bandini who planned to have another sculptor, Tiberio Calcagni, do the finishing work. However, Calcagni died a short time later and so the piece has Michelangelo's concept and Calcagni's partial finishing effort that can be seen on Mary Magdalene and the torso polishing of Christ. Calcagni was not nearly the level of artist that Michelangelo was, so it probably is better that the statue was not completed by him. The piece remained in Rome until 1674 when it was moved to San Lorenzo in Florence and then to the cathedral in 1722 where it remains to this day.

The *Rondanini Pieta*: 1545 to 1564

This *Pieta* is the last piece of artwork that Michelangelo ever worked on. It is another marble in the round. Just days before his death in 1564, he was seen chipping away on it by as described by his friend Daniele da Volterra in a letter to Michelangelo's nephew. The statue is even less finished than the *Florentine Pieta,* though it was probably started before it. After the frustration and damage to the *Florentine Pieta,* Michelangelo took up the carving of this unfinished piece which was probably started in 1545. As a result of reworking the concept, the statue is smaller than originally intended; this can be noticed by observing the unattached right arm of Christ that stands apart like a tree stump to the left side of the statue as it is seen. This piece was left to Michelangelo's assistant Antonio del Franzese. It spent many years in the Palazzo Rondanini in Rome, which name became attached to the piece. In 1952, it was purchased by the city of Milan and moved to the Sforza Castle in that city. The piece is 6 feet 3 inches in height.

The *Palestrina Pieta*: about 1550

This last Pieta subject has some doubters as to its true origins. Several art historians and researchers believe it is a Michelangelo while others believe it is a work of his followers based on his concept. Some believe it was started by Michelangelo and completed by assistants. There are no references to it in any of the contemporary sources so there is little to go on compared to the first two described in this section. It was apparently carved out of an old piece of Roman architecture as evidenced from the condition of the ornamentation on the back of the carving. It is made from material described as marble-like limestone. The use of this material seems to argue against it being done by the master. It can be seen today in the Accademia in Florence. Its name comes from the location in the chapel of the Palazzo of Barberini in Palestrina where it was seen for many years until purchased by the Italian government in 1939 and then moved to Florence.

Three figures make up the piece -- the body of the dead Christ as supported by his mother Mary and Mary Magdalene. The statue is

8 feet 2 inches high. Only Christ's face, torso and arm are even close to being finished. The other figures are only roughed out and need final sculpturing and polishing. These finishing touches may be what's needed to help to restore the proportions which seem to be a little out of balance. Perhaps the proportions being off slightly argue for the support that this was a not a sculpture by Michelangelo, but it was possibly done by his followers.

Picture 14-2. The *Palestrina Pieta.* It is now in the Accademia in Florence. It was located in Palestrina, Italy for many years, hence the name. (Alinari/Art Resource, NY)

CHAPTER 15

Michelangelo's Death and Burial--1564

The Last Trip to Florence

Michelangelo died on the 18th of February, 1564. He was just three weeks short of becoming 90 years old. This great artist had the attention of the most prominent people in Italy during his lifetime and that attention has now grown to include the whole world. Michelangelo's body was originally interred in the Santi Apostoli Church in Rome. This turned out to be a temporary arrangement; his brother secretly arranged for the body of Michelangelo to be moved to Florence. This was accomplished by hiding the body in a wagon load of merchandise to prevent any complications from the Roman authorities who did not want the remains moved.

Michelangelo's last trip to Florence ended March 10, 1564. His body was taken to his family parish, Santa Croce Church, in the same neighborhood where he lived earlier when in Florence. A memorial service was held for the great artist on July 14, 1564. Giorgio Vasari, the writer and artist, and a student of Michelangelo's, designed the tomb. It was not completed and dedicated until 1572. The tomb monument consists of three marble figures representing the three media in which Michelangelo worked; Painting, Sculpture and Architecture. These are seated at the foot of the coffin. There is also a marble bust of Michelangelo based on a Daniele da Volterra version which is mounted above the coffin. All are mounted on a simple catafalque which is about fifteen feet high. It is a fitting tribute to the artist who lived such a simple life while creating some of the greatest works of art that are still appreciated today. (See picture 15-1).

Picture 15-1   (Alinari/Art Resource, NY)
Michelangelo's tomb in Santa Croce in Florence. Giorgio Vasari, a friend and
student of Michelangelo's designed this memorial with the three figures of
Painting, Sculpture and Architecture. It was finally dedicated in 1572.

APPENDIXES:

A. Artists Who Preceded and Influenced Michelangelo and their
   Art Works

B. Locations Connected to Michelangelo in Italy

C. A Chronology of Michelangelo's Life and Activity

D. A Chronological List of Michelangelo's Artworks by Category

E. Bibliography of Books and Videos about Michelangelo

F. Maps

G. Index

Appendix A:

Artists who preceded Michelangelo and influenced his work:

1. **Architecture: (all locations are in Florence)**

Artist Name	Building	Date	Artistic Significance
Filippo Brunelleschi	Cathedral dome	1420- 1436	break-through design, inspired M in his design of St. Peter's dome in Rome.
F. Brunelleschi	Foundling Hospital	1444	great classical design for a public building which was 1st orphanage in Europe. strong influence on other architects.
F. Brunelleschi	San Lorenzo church	1421- 1469	simple and plain design, a new clean style and look.
Arnolfo di Cambio	Cathedral	1296 1294	replaced Santa Reparata; was one of largest and most important churches of time.
Giotto and Andrea Pisano	Baptistry	1294	major influence Renaissance architecture; mural inside on ceiling inspired all artists.
Giotto and Andrea Pisano	Cathedral Bell Tower	1334- 1355	stunning design, intricate use of marble.
Unknown	Ponte Vecchio	1345	the oldest bridge over the River Arno, crossed by M many times.
Leon Alberti	Sta. Maria Novella, facade	1357	frescoes by Masaccio, Ghirlandaio and Filippo Lippi.
Arnolfo di Cambio	Santa Croce	1294	Michelangelo's home church
F. Brunelleschi	Santa Spirito	1446	pleasing simple design and harmony where M studied anatomy.
Unknown	Orsanmichelle	1285- 1337	old grain market converted to church to honor Virgin Mary. Statues by Ghiberti, Donatello and Verrocchio, tabernacle by Orcagna.

Artists who preceded Michelangelo and influenced his work:
Architecture: (continued)

Artist Name	Building	Date	Artistic Significance
F. Brunelleschi	Santa Maria del Carmine church	1424	frescoes by Masaccio in the Brancacci Chapel.
Michelozzo	Medici Palace	1444-1464	Medici home, model for others, where M lived for 2 ½ years as a teenager.
Michelozzo and Alberti	San Marco Church	1437-1456	monastery is site of Fra Angelico frescoes.
Unknown	Bargello	1255	original city hall, later a prison, now a museum.
Arnolfo di Cambio and Michelozzo	City Hall (Palazzo Vecchio)	1310-1350	Powerful design of building symbolizes victory of civic harmony vs civil strife; has frescoes by Botticelli and Ghirlandaio.
Unknown	Ognissanti church	1480	*Madonna* painted by Ghirlandaio, also *Last Supper* in Refectory.
Unknown	San Miniato al Monte church	1018-1062	major Romanesque influence on Renaissance architecture, especially for Sta. Maria Novella church.
F. Brunelleschi and Giuliano da Maiano	Pazzi Chapel in Santa Croce	1440-1461	masterpiece of architecture design with graceful proportions and spaces.
	Plazza della Signoria	1299	main square in Florence in front of Palazzo Vecchio, site of many public events.
Simone Talenti	Loggia dei Lanzia	1383	Large covered area used for displays of sculptures, located across from City Hall on Plazza della Signoria.
Leon Alberti	Rucellai Palace	1456	ornate architectural design, now used as a museum of photography.

2. **Painting that influenced Michelangelo:**

Artist Name	Painting	Date	Location and Significance
Masaccio	*Tribute Money*	1420-1427	in Brancacci Chapel at Santa Maria del Carmine, first three dimensional realism with applied use of perspective.
Ghirlandaio	*Life of the Virgin* *Life of St. John*	1478	Santa Maria Novella church; he was strong advocate of drawing before starting the painting; had life-long influence on M. Allowed apprentices to assist him in fresco painting jobs.
Luca Signorelli	frescoes	1490	Cathedral at Orvieto; an early great painter of nude figures in motion. Inspired M's *Last Judgement* fresco.
Giotto	*Life of St. Francis*	1317	Bardi Chapel in Santa Croce church; new use of light and shadow techniques.
Giotto	*Ascension of St. John the Baptist*	1320	Peruzzi Chapel in Santa Croce church; inspired figure drawing by M.
Botticelli	*Primavera* and *Birth of Venus*	1480 1485	Ufizzi Museum; new use of pigments and colors in classical mythology themes.
Fra Angelico	*Annunciation* and *Crucifixion*	1445 1442	San Marco Church; new use of perspective and expression of emotion.

3. Sculpture that influenced Michelangelo:

Artist Name	Sculpture	Date	Location and Significance
Donatello	St. Mark	1412	Orsanmichele; highly
	St. George	1416	admired by Michelangelo
	David	1430	and other artists.
Verrocchio	Child and Dolphin	1475	Palazzo Vecchio and Orsanmichele; strong sense
	David	1475	of movement and vitality;
	Doubting Thomas	1465	dynamic design.
Ghiberti	Doors of Baptistry	1403-1452	Baptistry in Florence; outstanding reliefs; M called them Gates of Paradise.
Antonio Pollaiuolo	Hercules and Anteaus	1470	Bargello in Florence; an early action group.
Nicola Pisano	Pulpit reliefs	1260	Baptistry in Pisa; reliefs are similar to ancient Roman sarcophagus carvings.
Giovanni Pisano	marble pulpit	1298	Sant' Andrea church in Pistoia; marble pulpit depicts dynamic action in the figures.
Luca della Robia	roundels	1450	Hospital of the Innocents in Florence; glazed terra-cotta moldings in the round.
Jacopo della Quercia	Creation of Adam Expulsion Temptation	1425-1438	Carved doorway reliefs at Saint Petronio in Bologna: studied by 19 year old M; Jacopo was a pioneer of great action figures in relief.
	Fonte Gaia	1419	Fountain with reliefs in Piazza del Campo in Siena.
Andrea Pisano	marble reliefs	1334-1348	Duomo Campanile in Florence; admired by M.

Appendix B:

Places to see that have a connection to Michelangelo and what to see there:

Location	Significance	What to see there related to Michelangelo
Florence	Where M lived and and worked from 1485 to 1532;	Buonarroti home at Via Bentacordi No. 7

Medici Palace and Gardens on Via Larga

Santa Maria Novella Church: M worked here as an apprentice

Santa Croce Church-Michelangelo's tomb

San Lorenzo Church

San Marco Church

Santa Trinita Church

S Annunziata Church

Bargello Museum: *Bacchus, Pitti Madonna, Apollo, Brutus*

Palazzo Vecchio (City Hall); *Victory*

Library of San Lorenzo and entry room w/stairs

Medici Chapel at San Lorenzo with Medici tombs; hidden room below altar with charcoal drawings done while he was in hiding in 1530, *Madonna and Child* marble sculpture.

Santa Maria del Carmine--Brancacci Chapel

Hill of San Miniato; site of M's earthen fortifications and memorial statue to M overlooking Florence.

Casa Buonarroti--museum with many M items: *Madonna of the Stairs, Battle of the Centaurs, Wooden Crucifix,* many drawings.

Santa Maria del Fiore (Cathedral), St. Matthew statue, pavement design around chair of Cathedral in red, white and black marble.

Santa Trinita Bridge--M designed with fellow architect Ammanati

Academia--*David* and *Four Captives* on display; unfinished *St Matthew, Palestrina Pieta.*

Uffizi Museum; *Doni Holy Family* tondo

Opera del Duomo--*Florentine Pieta*

Location	Significance	What to see there related to Michelangelo
Settignano	Site of family farm near Florence	Where M went to escape the pressures of Florence. Raised as a child here until about 10 years old with a stone cutter's family.
Caprese	Born here in 1475	Building where M was born, Chapel where M was baptized, museum about M.
Carrara	Site of marble quarry and docks	M's favorite source for high quality marble. Large port facility to ship marble
Seravezza	Site of marble quarry	The Pope told M to use marble from here
Pietrasanta	Site of marble quarry	The Pope told M to use marble from here
Pisa and Genoa	Source of boats for shipping marble	Visited by M to arrange for boats to ship marble to Florence and Rome
Siena	Contains M's work in Piccolomini altar	St. Dominic's Church statues
Venice	Two trips by M	Trips in 1494 and 1529 to flee Florence. See Rialto Bridge, St. Mark's Square and Church, and Doges Palace. M was there.
Ferrara	Trip by M to visit Duke Alfonso d'Este	See moated fortress castle of d'Este and fortification walls at edge of town studied by M.
Poggibonsi	Small town south of Florence	M passed through often on way to Siena and Rome. Stopped here by Papal Guard after fleeing Rome and Pope Julius II in 1506.
Bologna	Where M had first job	Commissioned by Aldovrandi to do statues of four saints for St. Domenico Church and a Kneeling Angel. Studied works of Jacapo della Quercia on facade of St. Petrinius.

Location	Significance	What to see there related to Michelangelo
Rome	Where M had a lot of work	Lived in home of Cardinal Riario (now the Chancelleria)
		Palazzo Farnese; M assisted in design of third floor, windows and cornice
		Campidoglio; M designed the courtyard, the steps to the Senatorial Palace, the facade of Palace of the Conservatori building and the museum building across from it. M also did the design of the pedestal under the statue of Marcus Aurelius.
		St. Peter's Basilica; M completed the work on the main church and added the dome.
		The Pieta sculpture is in the Basilica.
		Santa Maria sopra Minerva; *Risen Christ*
		St. Peter in Chains: Tomb of Pope Julius II with *Moses* and *Rachel and Leah.*
		St. Silvestro al Quirinale Church where M would visit with Vittoria Colonna
		Castel Sant' Angelo where M had a workshop for awhile and where he designed the facade of Pope Leo X's chapel.
		The Vatican apartments: Cappella Pauline-- two frescoes: *Crucifixion of St Peter* and *Conversion of St. Paul* (private)
		Sistine Chapel: ceiling fresco of Creation and other bible events; fresco wall over altar depicting *The Last Judgement.*
		Vatican; Belvedere Niche stairs
		Porta Pia; gateway designed by M.
		Santa Maria degli Angeli Church: M designed conversion from Baths of Diocletian

Appendix C:
A chronology of Michelangelo's life and activity by Location:

Date	Location	Activity
6 Mar., 1475	Caprese	M is born while father is mayor here for six months.
April 1475	Caprese	M is baptized at Church of Santo Giovanni.
April 1475	Caprese-Florence	Buonarroti family returns to Florence.
April 1475	Settignano	M is sent to live with wet nurse in a family of stone workers. His own mother is too frail.
1481	Florence	M's mother dies.
1485	Florence	M rejoins family in Florence.
	Florence	M's father Lodovico marries Lucrezia Ubaldini. Family is living in house on Via dei Bentacordi No. 7.
1486	Florence	Francesco da Urbino becomes M's tutor for study of Humanities. Shows more interest in drawing and sketching. Meets life-long friend Granacci.
1 April 1488	Florence	M joins the studio of Domenico Ghirlandaio. Learns to draw and paint frescoes. Studies earlier painters

Giotto in the Peruzzi Chapel in Santa Croce
Masaccio in the Brancacci Chapel in Santa
Maria del Carmine.
Major contemporary architecture and art for
M that still exists:
Church: Santa Maria Novella
Church: San Marco
Church: San Lorenzo
Church: SS. Annuziata
Church: Santa Maria del Carmine
Palace: Medici Palazzo
Baptistery
Cathedral: The Duomo
Bell Tower
The Bargello
Church: Or San Michele
Palace: Palazzo della Signoria (City Hall)
Loggia dei Lanzi in Palazzo della Signoria

Date	Location	Activity
		Church: Santa Croce
		Bridge: Ponte Vecchio
		Artists with Influence on M:
		Masaccio: started the Renaissance. Influenced M in his work in the Sistine Chapel.
		Brunelleschi: developed perspective
		Giotto: brought feeling of flesh and blood to human forms
		Ghiberti who trained Donatello who revived classical sculptor of the human body and taught Bertoldo di Giovanni, M's teacher
		Ghirlandaio
		Luca Signorelli
		Antonio Pollaiolo - nude sketches
		Giovanni Pisano
		Jacopo della Quercia in Siena
		Luca della Robia
1488-89	Florence	M works as assistant to Ghirlandaio on frescoes on *Life of the Virgin Mary* and *Life of St. John the Baptist* in the Choir of Santa Maria Novella.
March 1489	Florence	M joins the Medici studio run by aging Bertoldo di Giovanni to study sculpture near Medici palace. Gets nose broken by Torrigiani later that year.
1490	Florence	Draws from Masaccio's *Tribute Money*. Now in Munich.
Summer 1490	Florence	M carves a marble study of an **Ancient Faun**. First known carving of M. Now lost. Lorenzo Medici asks M to become part of his household.
1491	Florence	M carves **Madonna of the Stairs**. Now in Casa Buonarroti. Bertoldo dies.
1492	Florence	M carves the **Battle of the Centaurs**. Now in Casa Buonarroti.

Date	Location	Activity
8 April 1492	Florence	Lorenzo Medici dies. M returns to home of his father.
1492	Florence	Piero Medici invited M to live at the Palace. No assignments were given by Piero to M except a snowman to celebrate a rare snow.
1492-1493	Florence	Santo Spirito Hospital and Church: M studies human anatomy by dissecting cadavers to be buried. M carves **Wooden Crucifix** as "thank you" to the Prior. Now in Casa B. Was lost from early 1800's till 1963.
1493	Florence	M carves **Hercules** for experience. Strozzi family buys it. Later sells it to King Francis I of France. Lost after 1731.
Oct. 1494	Venice & Bologna	M goes to Bologna by way of Venice to flee impending overthrow of Piero. Piero is ousted in Nov.
Nov. 1494	Bologna	M meets new mentor: Giovanni Francesco Aldovrandi.
1495	Bologna	M carves three statues for Church of Santo Domenico: **St. Petronius, St. Proculus, Kneeling Angel**
late 1495	Florence	M returns to Florence. A Medici relative commissions marble carving of **St. John the Baptist**. Now lost.
early 1496	Florence	M carves antique style of **Reclining Cupid** at suggestion from Piero Medici. Was falsely sold to Cardinal Raffaello Riario in Rome by Baldassare as an antique. Last seen in Whitehall in England 1698.
1496	Florence	**Youthful St. John,** now lost.
25 June 1496	Rome	M moves to Rome at urging of Pope's emissary Leo Baglioni. Lives in Cardinal's home, now the Chancelleria.
Summer 1496	Rome	Banker Jacapo Galli commissions statue of **Apollo**, now lost. Also **Bacchus**, now in Museo Nazionale del Bargello in Florence. Galli introduces M to French Cardinal Jean Villiers de Lagraulas who discusses the *Pieta*.

Date	Location	Activity
Dec. 1497 to March 1498	Carrara	M obtaining marble for the Pieta
27 Aug. 1498	Rome	Finally signs the contract for the Pieta
Spring 1499	Rome	**Pieta** completed. Now in St. Peter's Basilica.
1500	Rome	Starts to paint **Entombment**, not finished, now in London at National Gallery. On loan to Florence 10-99 to 2-00 for special exhibit on M.
May 1501	Florence	M returns to Florence since there is no work in Rome.
19 June 1501	Florence	M signs contract for Cardinal Piccolomini tomb in Siena for 15 Statues, who later is Pope Pius III. Pope is buried in Rome so tomb becomes an altar
16 Aug. 1501	Florence	M receives contract to carve the David.
1501 to 1504	Florence	M carves the **David**. Work shop at the Office of the Works of the Duomo, Santa Maria del Fiori, behind the Cathedral
12 Aug. 1505	Florence	M receives commission to do **Bronze David** for Pierre de Rohan, Marechal de Gie.
May 1504	Florence	Marble **David** is set up in the Piazza Vecchio. Now in the Academia.
1501--1504	Siena Trips	M works on contract for Piccolomini family for cardinal's tomb. Four of 15 statues completed. Carved in Florence **St. Francis**, **St. Peter**, **Gregory the Great**, **Pope Pius I**
1503	Florence	M's workshop at corner of Borgo Pinti and Via della Colonna built for him by Cathedral Board of works.
24 April 1503	Florence	M receives contract for 12 apostles for the Duomo.
1504	Florence	M completes the **Mouscron Madonna**, now in Notre Dame church in Bruges. Was originally for the Piccolomini tomb in Siena.
1504	Florence	M does the **Taddei Madonna** in round marble for Taddei family. Now in Royal Academy in London.

Date	Location	Activity
		M does the **Doni Holy Family** tondi painting for Doni family. Now in the Uffizi.
		M does the **Pitti Madonna** tondi in marble for the Pitti family. Now in the Bargello.
		M works on cartoon for **Battle of Cascina**.
March 1505	Rome	M summoned to Rome by Pope Julius II. Pope's **Tomb** designed with 40 statutes.
April-Dec. 1505	Carrara	M in quarries getting marble for the tomb statues for Pope Julius II.
Jan. 1506	Rome	M sets up small workshop in Castel Sant Angelo so Pope can easily visit him. May also have established a workshop at Market of Crows near Piazza Venezia. Latter was destroyed by the erection of the Victor Emanuelle II monument in 1880's. M carves **4 Slaves** and the **Moses** for the tomb. Now in Accademia in Florence and the Moses now in St. Peter's in Chains in Rome.
27 Jan 1506	Rome	M buys farm at San Stefano a Pozzolatico near Florence.
17 April 1506	Florence	M flees to Florence when Pope refuses to get current on the expenses for the tomb. Works on **St. Matthew** for the Cathedral and on **Battle of Cascina.**
29 Nov. 1506	Bologna	M meets Pope Julius II in Bologna to resolve their dispute. Meet in San Petrina and Palazzo de' Sedici. M receives commission from Pope to do a bronze casting of him.
1507	Bologna	M working on casting molds in studio behind San Petronio. Buys farm in Settignano.
Spring 1507	Bologna	M trying to find good casters for the statue.
July 1507	Bologna	M achieves good casting with 2nd attempt.
March 1508	Bologna	**Pope Julius II bronze casting** is completed. Destroyed Dec. 30, 1511 by rioters.
9 March 1508	Florence	M starts again on the 12 apostles. Buys house on Via Ghibellina, now Casa Buonarroti. Unfinished **St. Matthew** now in Accademia.

Date	Location	Activity
18 March 1508	Florence	M rents new house and workshop on Borgo Pinti built by the Cathedral Board of Works
April 1508	Rome	M called to Rome by Pope. Assignment: Paint ceiling of the **Sistine Chapel**.
May 10 1508	Rome	M signs contract and starts the painting of the **Sistine Chapel**, original design.
June 1508	Rome	M signs new contract with final design for **Sistine Chapel**.
26 Dec. 1508	Rome	**Bronze David** is shipped to France. Benedetto da Rovenzanno finished it for M in Florence.
Sept. 25, 1510	Bologna & Florence	M goes to see the Pope to get paid. Goes thru Florence to visit family on way to Bologna
Oct. 1510	Rome	M returns to Rome.
Dec. 1510	Bologna	M goes to see the Pope 2nd time to get paid.
Jan. 1511	Rome	M returns to Rome. Starts work on 3rd section of ceiling. Main workshop moved from Castel Sant' Angelo to location in Marcel de' Corvi (Market of the Crows), a small street near the Capitoline Hill near Trajan's Column. Destroyed when Victor Emanuelle II monument was built.
14 Aug 1511	Rome	**Sistine Chapel** unveiled without lunettes painted.
1512	Florence	M bought an estate in Santo Stefano in Pane near Florence.
1 Nov. 1512	Rome	Completed **Sistine Chapel** is unveiled.
1513--1516	Rome	Works on Statues for Pope Julius II tomb, **Moses** and **Two Slaves.**
1513	Rome	Pope dies 21 Feb, 1513. 6 May new contract for the tomb signed with Pope's executors
14 June 1514	Rome	Contract for **Resurrected Christ** for Santa Maria sopra Minerva. First attempt failed due to bad vein in marble.
Aug/Sept 1515	Carrara	New contract for Pope Julius's Tomb agreed to. M went to Carrara to select marbles.
1516	Rome	M also designs a **front of Leo X Chapel** in marble in the Castel Sant' Angelo.

Date	Location	Activity
May 12, 1516	Florence	M called to Florence by Pope Leo X to work on the projects for the Medici family: the **Medici Chapel** and **facade** of **San Lorenzo**. Workshop is in Via San Zanobi.
Fall 1516	Carrara	M makes several trips to obtain marbles.
Dec. 1516	Rome	Presents facade drawing of San Lorenzo to Pope Leo X.
Spring 1517	Florence	M worked on Medici projects. a trip or two to Carrara
Summer 1517	Florence	M completes the **wooden model** of the **facade** of the church of **San Lorenzo**
1517	Florence	Designs **windows** on ground floor for Medici Palace.
January 1518	Rome	Signed new contract with Pope.
Feb 6, 1518	Florence	M closed workshop in Rome and went to Florence. Sent marbles for Julius tomb to Florence to work on there.
1518	Florence	M bought house on Via San Zanobi. (Via Mozza then) Used as workshop for Facade of San Lorenzo and Tomb of Julius II.
Early 1518	Florence	Pope Leo X insists M get marbles from Pietrasanta and Seravezza in Territory of Florence; Carrara is outside Pope's control.
Sept. 1518	Seravezza	M working on getting more marbles for tomb.
Dec. 21, 1518	Florence	M carving tomb statues. Buys house at S. Pier Maggiore.
Feb. 25, 1519	Pietrasanta & Seravezza	M assisting in road construction to get marbles to ships.
March 20, 1519	Florence	M returns to Florence. Has new block of marble for **Resurrected Christ**.
March 1519	Genoa	M goes to Genoa to obtain barges for the marbles.
April 1519	Pisa	M goes to Pisa to get more barges for the marbles.
March 1520	Florence	Contract for facade for San Lorenzo is canceled by Pope. Money to go to new Medici Chapel and tombs instead.

Date	Location	Activity
1519-1520	Florence	M carves **Christ of Resurrection.** It is installed in Rome after some delay in March 1521. Now in Santa Maria Sopra Minerva in Rome.
Dec 1520	Florence	M completes model for Medici Chapel.
April 1521	Carrara	M travels to get more marbles for the Medici Chapel.
Oct. 1521	Florence	M visits with his father in Settignano. Works on Medici tomb.
Dec. 1523	Rome	M called to Rome by Pope Clement VII.
Jan. 1524	Florence	Pope assigns M to lead all Medici projects in Florence: The **Medici Library**, the **Tombs,. the New Sacristy.** This confirms M as the pre-eminent artist in Florence.
March 1524	Florence	The site is chosen for the Medici Library.
Spring 1524	Florence	Wooden model for Medici Chapel for the Tombs is completed.
1525	Rome	M works on the Library and Chapel marbles.
1526	Florence	M works in Florence.
May 1527	Rome/Florence	Rome is sacked by Spanish. Work stops. Pope hides in Castel Sant' Angelo. M flees to Florence.
1527 to 1528	Florence	M carves **Victory.** Now in Palazzo Vecchio.
1528	Florence	Commissioned by Capponi to carve **Hercules/Sampson.**
Oct. 1528	Florence	M employed as fortifications expert by Capponi to protect Florence.
1529	Florence	M helps **design of fortifications** on Hill of San Miniato.
April 1529	Florence	City Council elects M Governor and Procruator General of the fortifications for Florence
June 1529	Pisa and Livorno	M evaluates their fortifications for ideas.
July 1529	Ferrara	M visits this city to examine the fortifications for ideas. Stays at castle of Duke d'Este **Leda and the Swan** painting commissioned by Duke of Ferrara, Alfonso I d'Este.

Date	Location	Activity
Sept 21, 1529	Venice	M flees to Venice with three friends. His fortification work was against the new Republic. Submits design for new **Rialto Bridge**. Now lost. Awarded to another.
Nov 23, 1529	Florence	M back in Florence working on **fortification designs** on Hill of San Miniato.
August 1529	Florence	Papal commissioner orders M's assassination
Sept. 1530	Florence	M is in hiding while city is controlled by Spanish for a few weeks. Hides in **Crypt** under the altar in Medici Chapel. Draws on walls with charcoal.
Oct. 1530	Florence	M starts carving **Apollo** for Baccio Valori as "thank you" for the pardon received in Florence. Now in Bargello.
Oct/Nov 1530	Florence	M is pardoned by the Pope and allowed to continue work on the statues for the Medici Chapel at San Lorenzo Church.
Late 1530	Florence	M paints the **Leda and the Swan** for Duke Alfonso I d'Este. Never delivered to the Duke. Now lost.
1530	Florence	M completes **Victory** statue for the Tomb.
Early 1531	Florence	M's father Lodovico dies. M works on Medici Chapel statues. M sick himself from exhaustion.
June 1531	Florence	**Aurora** finished. Part of Medici tombs.
August 1531	Florence	**Notte** finished. Part of Medici tombs.
November 1531	Florence	**Leda and Swan** painting given to pupil and friend of M, Antonio Mini. Now lost.
1531 - 1532	Florence	M carves **Reliquary Tribune** for San Lorenzo.
April 1532	Rome	M goes to Rome to sign a new contract for the Tomb for Pope Julius II. Now only six statues needed, down from original forty.
May 1532	Florence	M returns to work on Tomb statues and Medici Chapel.
1532	Florence	M does drawing of **Andrea Quaratesi.** now in London.

Date	Location	Activity
Fall/Winter-- 1532/33	Rome	M makes several trips to Rome to check progress on the tomb. Meets Tommaso Cavalieri. Becomes life-long friend.
June 1533	Florence	Working on Medici Chapel, Library, **Victory,** (now in Palazzo Vecchio) and **Four Slaves** (now in Accademia)
Sept 22, 1533	San Miniato Al Tedesco	M meets with Pope Clement VII as Pope was on his way to Marseilles.
October 1533	Rome	M returns. Starts discussion with Pope Clement VII on **Resurrection** painting for Sistine Chapel wall over the altar.
May 1534	Florence	M working on various projects.
Sept. 23, 1534	Rome	Two days after M arrives in Rome, Pope Clement VII dies. M spends rest of his life living and working in Rome. He left a statue of a **Madonna** in Florence that was designed for the Tomb. M gets started on design of public buildings.
1534	Rome	New Pope, Pope Paul III is elected. He commissions M to paint the Frescos above the Altar in the Sistine Chapel. Results in **The Last Judgement.**
Sept. 1, 1535	Rome	M is appointed Chief Painter, Architect and Sculptor for the Vatican Palace.
April 1536	Rome	M starts **The Last Judgement** on new brick and plaster wall at end of Sistine Chapel.
1536/38	Rome	M meets Vittoria Colonna
1537	Rome	M starts on designs for Campidoglio.
1538	Rome	M designs **base** for **Marcus Aurelius** Statue and moves the statue to the square in front of the Senatorial Palace.
1540's	Rome	M and Vittoria Collona meet at church of S. Silvestro al Quirinale to hear readings on the letters of St. Paul.
Oct. 31, 1541	Rome	M completes **The Last Judgement.** During these 5 ½ years he vacations in Tivoli at Villa d'Este.

Date	Location	Activity
1542	Rome	M starts the bust of **Brutus**, finished by Tiberio Calcagni. Now in Bargello in Florence
20 Aug 1542	Rome	Final contract change for Pope Julius tomb; now only 3 statues from Michelangelo.
1542	Rome	M completes **Rachel** and **Leah** for Pope Julius tomb with help from Raffaello da Montelupo.
1544	Rome	M designs tomb for nephew in Santa Maria Arncaeli, executed by M's assistant, Urbino.
1544-1546	Rome	M is frequently sick in this period. Lives with Luigi Del Riccio at Strozzi home in Rome.
3 Feb 1545	Rome	Pope Julius II Tomb itself is finally completed. M's statues **Moses, Rachel** and **Leah** placed on Tomb.
1545	Rome	M working on two frescoes in Pope's private chapel, Cappella Paolina, **Conversion of St. Paul** and **Crucifixion of St. Peter.**
July 1545	Rome	**Conversion of St. Paul** finished.
1546	Rome	M starts design work on **Capitoline Hill**. Palazzo Senatorio steps.
20 March, 1546	Rome	M becomes a citizen of Rome.
1546	Rome	M works on design of **Palazzo Farnese**, 3rd floor windows and cornice.
Nov. 1546	Rome	Accepts commission from Pope Paul III to take over building of new St. Peter's Basilica.
1547	Rome	Vittoria Colonna dies. M working on Vatican fortifications.
		M begins work on another marble **Pieta** sculpture intended for his own tomb. (now in Cathedral in Florence). Includes Joseph of Arimathea as M's own self portrait.
Fall 1547	Rome	Completes **wooden model** of St. Peter's basilica. Now in Vatican.
1548 to 1556	Rome	M works on his **Pieta**, now in the Duomo in Florence.
1549-1550	Rome	Designs ceiling, floor and desks for **Medici Library** in Florence.
March 1550	Rome	**Crucifixion of St. Peter** completed.

Date	Location	Activity
1550's	Rome	M works on design for **San Giovanni dei Fiorentini** in Rome. It was not completed. Plans now in Casa Buonarroti in Florence.
1550 -- 1551	Rome	M works on the design for the stairway design for the **Belvedere Niche** in the Vatican Gardens.
1550 to 1556	Rome	M designs **Florentine Pieta** with four figures, now in Mus. Opera del Duomo in Florence
1554	Rome	M provides design ideas for Il Gesu, the new Jesuit Church
Sept 1555	Rome	Designs **Stairway** for **Medici Library** in Florence.
1556	Rome	Papal wars stop work on St. Peter's.
1556	Rome	M carves the **Palestrina Pieta**, now in Academia in Florence, finished by a pupil
1556 to 1564	Rome	M carves the **Rondanini Pieta**, his last statue. Now in Milan in Sforza Castle
Oct 1556	Spoleto	M flees Rome to go to Loreto when Spanish army threatens; gets as far as Spoleto before being recalled.
1560	Rome	M resigns as chief architect of St. Peter's.
1558 to 1561	Rome	M makes **Wooden Model** of dome for St. Peter's. Construction of **Dome** was completed by Giacomo della Porta in 1588. t
1559	Rome	M. designs for **Sforza Chapel** in Santa Maria Maggiore.
1561	Rome	Designs a partial plan for the rebuilding of the great hall of the Baths of Diocletian for **Santa Maria degli Angeli**.
1561 to 1565	Rome	M designs **Porta Pia**, commissioned by Pope Pius IV
1562	Rome	M is replaced as Supreme Overseer for St. Peter's. He confronts the Pope, Pius IV and is reinstated.
18 Feb 1564	Rome	M dies. 3 weeks short of 90 years old at home in Macel de Corvi. Originally buried in Santi Apostoli in Rome.
21 Feb. 1564	Rome	M is secretly moved to Florence hidden in a wagon load of merchandise by his brother.

Date	Location	Activity
10 March 1564	Florence	M's body arrives in Florence at Santa Croce.
14 July 1564	Florence	Memorial service for M in Santa Croce.
1572	Florence	M.'s tomb completed and dedicated. Designed by Vasari, one of his pupils. 3 figures on the tomb; Painting, Sculpture and Architecture plus bust of M.

Appendix D: Chronological list of Michelangelo's Art Works

SCULPTURE:
Note: Sources used don't all agree on some items * if Michelangelo did the sculpture or if his followers or other sculptors did it. Sources also don't agree on dates: there is as much as 14 years difference in the dates. Sculpture sources: Umberto Baldini, Frederick Hartt, Ludwig Goldscheider, Linda Murray.

Item Description	Date	Present Location
Head of a Faun	1489	Now Lost
Madonna Della Scala	1491	Florence, Casa Buonarroti
Battle of the Lapiths & Centaurs	1492	Florence, Casa Buonarroti
Santo Spirito Crucifix	1493	Florence, Casa Buonarroti
Hercules	1493	Now Lost
St. Proclus	1495	Bologna, San Domenico
St. Petronius	1495	Bologna, San Domenico
Kneeling Angel	1495	Bologna, San Domenico
Bacchus	1497	Florence, Bargello Nat'l Museum
Youthful St. John	1496	Now Lost
Sleeping Cupid	1496	Now Lost
Cupid/Apollo	1497	Now Lost
Pieta	1500	Rome, St. Peter's Basilica
St. Paul *	1501	Siena, Duomo
St. Peter *	1502	Siena, Duomo
Taddei Tondi	1502	London, Royal Academy
St. Pius *	1503	Siena, Duomo
St. Gregory *	1504	Siena Duomo
Bruges Madonna and Child	1504	Bruges, Notre Dame
David	1504	Florence, Academy of Fine Arts
Pitti Tondi	1505	Florence, Bargello Nat'l Museum
St. Matthew	1506	Florence, Academy of Fine Arts
David (bronze)	1508	Now Lost
Julius II (Bronze)	1508	Bologna, destroyed 1511
Dying Slave	1513	Paris, Louvre
Rebel Slave	1513	Paris, Louvre
Moses	1515	Rome, San Pietro in Vincoli
The Risen Christ Holding the Cross	1520	Rome, Santa Maria sopra Minerva
River God (clay)	1525	Florence, Academy of Fine Arts

Item Description	Date	Present Location
Hercules/Sampson (clay)	1528	Florence, Casa Buonarroti
Crouching Youth*	1530	Leningrad, The Hermitage Mus.
Young Prisoner (Beardless Slave)	1530	Florence, Academy of Fine Arts
Victory	1531	Florence, Palazzo Vecchio
David/Apollo	1532	Florence, Bargello National Mus.
Bearded Prisoner (Bearded Slave)	1533	Florence, Academy of Fine Arts
Reawakening Prisoner (Cross-legged Slave)	1533	Florence, Academy of Fine Arts
Atlas Prisoner (Blockhead Slave)	1533	Florence, Academy of Fine Arts
Medici Madonna	1534	Florence, The Medici Chapel in San Lorenzo
Twilight	1534	Florence, The Medici Chapel in San Lorenzo
Dawn	1534	Florence, The Medici Chapel in San Lorenzo
Night	1534	Florence, The Medici Chapel in San Lorenzo
Day	1534	Florence, The Medici Chapel in San Lorenzo
Giuliano de Medici	1534	Florence, The Medici Chapel
Lorenzo de Medici	1534	Florence, The Medici Chapel
Rachel (Contemplative Life) for Julius II Tomb	1542	Rome, San Pietro in Vincoli
Leah (Active Life) for Julius II Tomb	1542	Rome, San Pietro in Vincoli
Brutus	1542	Florence, Bargello National Mus.
Florentine Pieta	1448-1555	Florence, Mus. Opera del Duomo Santa Maria del Fiore Cathedral
Palestrina Pieta	1556	Florence, Academy of Fine Arts
Wooden Model for Crucifix	1562	Florence, Casa Buonarroti
Rondanini Pieta	1555-1564	Milan, Sforza Castle Civic Mus.

ARCHITECTURE:

Note: Many of these items, designed by M were not completed until after his death. Some designs were never executed, e.g. Facade of San Lorenzo.

Item Description	Date	Present Location
Front of Small Chapel Angelo	1516	Rome, Castel Sant'
North Portal of S. Apollonia Church	1517	Florence
Facade for San Lorenzo (wooden model) Buonarroti	1518	Florence, Casa
Windows on Medici Palace	1520	Florence, Medici Palace
Floor design at chair in Duomo	1524	Florence, Cathedral
Lorenzo Medici Library (vestibule, steps and reading room)	1524	Florence, Medici Lib.
Fortifications at San Miniato	1529	Florence, San Miniato
Pergamo of San Lorenzo (Sacrarium)	1532	Florence, San Lorenzo
Medici Chapel at San Lorenzo	1534	Florence, San Lorenzo
Base for Marcus Aurelius statute	1539	Rome, Piazza del Campidoglio
Tomb of Cechino Bracci	1545	Rome, Santa Maria in Aracaeli
Tomb of Pope Julius II	1505--1545	Rome, San Pietro in Vincoli
Piazza of the Capitol	1546	Rome
St. Peter's Basilica	1546+	Rome, The Vatican
Palazzo Farnese, Interior Courtyard 3rd floor and outside cornice design	1547	Rome
Coat of Arms, Palazzo Farnese	1550	Rome
Window over entry, Palazzo Farnese	1550	Rome
Belvedere Niche Stairway	1551	Rome, The Vatican
Steps of Palazzo dei Senatorio	1552	Rome, Piazza del Campidoglio
Wooden Model for Dome of St. Peter's	1561	Rome, The Vatican
Porta Pia	1561	Rome
Conversion of Baths of Diocletian to Church of Santa Maria degli Angeli	1563	Rome
Palazzo dei Conservatori	>1564	Rome, Piazza del Campidoglio

PAINTINGS AND DRAWINGS: (a selection) (P = painting, D = drawing)

Item Description	Date	Present Location
D Drawing of St. Peter after Masaccio in pen	1490	Munich, Graphische Sammlung
D The Ascension of the Evangelist (Copy of Giotto's fresco in Santa Croce)	1491?	Paris, Louvre
P Manchester Madonna	1498	London, National Gallery
P The Deposition (Entombment)	1498	London, National Gallery
D Study for a hand, leg and back of male	1499	Florence, Casa Buonarroti
D Study for Bronze David in pen	1501	Paris, Louvre
D Virgin and Child with St. Anne in pen	1502	Oxford, Ashmolean Museum
D Study for Monumental David in pen & ink	1502	Paris, Louvre
P Doni Madonna Tondi	1503	Florence, Uffizi Museum
D Studies of nude and draped figures in pen	1503	Chantilly, Musee Conde
D Three Draped Men after Masaccio	1503	Vienna, Albertina
D Study of Madonna and Child in black chalk and pen	1504	London, British Museum
D Group of 3 figures for Battle of Cascina, pencil, pen and ink	1504	Paris, Louvre
D Study for Battle of Cascina in black chalk	1504	Vienna, Albertina
D Cartoon for the Battle of Cascina	1505	Florence, Uffizi Museum
D Study of nude bathers in cartoon for Battle of Cascina in pen and brush in two ink colors	1505	London, British Museum
D Virgin and Child with St. Anne, pen and brown ink, brown wash and graphite	1505	Paris, Louvre
D Studies of Nudes for Cartoon	1505	Florence, Uffizi Museum
P Sistine Chapel	1508-1512	Rome, The Vatican
D Studies of cornice and nudes for Sistine Ch.	1508	Florence, Casa Buonarroti

Item Description	Date	Present Location
D Study of figure for Sistine Ch.	1508	Florence, Casa Buonarroti
D Study of Ignudi figures for Sistine Chapel	1508	London, British Museum
D Study of head in red pencil	1508	Florence, Casa Buonarroti
D Study in red of foreshortened head	1508	Florence, Casa Buonarroti
D Sketch for Sistine Chapel: hand and torso in pen black chalk	1509	Detroit, Institute of Arts
D Sketch for Sistine Chapel in pen and bl. chalk	1509	London, British Museum
D Studies for Eve in Expulsion, in red chalk	1510	Vienna, Albertina
D Studies for the Execution of Haman in Sistine Chapel in red chalk	1511	London, British Museum
D Study of the Libyan Sibyl in red chalk	1511	New York, Metropolitan Mus.
D Bistre sketch for Resurrection study	1512	Windsor, Royal Library
D Red pencil sketch for Resurrection of Christ		Paris, Louvre
D Design for Tomb of Julius II, pen & ink, wash	1513	Florence, Uffizi Museum
D Study for Putto, Libyan Sibyl, Tomb of Julius. red chalk, pen and ink	1514	Oxford, Ashmolean Museum
D The Flagellation in red chalk	1516	London, British Museum
D The Risen Lazarus in red chalk	1516	London, British Museum
D Drawing for Facade of San Lorenzo, red chalk and Charcoal	1517	Florence, Casa Buonarroti
D Sketch for a double tomb	1521	London, British Museum
D Study for Night for Medici Tomb, pen & ink	1521	Florence, Uffizi Museum

Item Description	Date	Present Location
D Study for a reading desk, Laurentian Library pen and red chalk	1524	Florence, Casa Buonarroti
D Study for Library portal, pen	1524	London, British Museum
D Sketch for Library stairs and base profiles, pen, red and black chalks	1525	Florence, Casa Buonarroti
D Study for River God in pen and ink	1525	London, British Museum
D Mural drawings on crypt walls of New Sacristy	1529	Florence, San Lorenzo
D Fortifications of Florence, pen and red chalk	1529	Florence, Casa Buonarroti
D Portrait of Andrea Quaratesi	1532	London, British Museum
D The Rape of Granymede in black chalk	1532	Windsor, Royal Library
D The Punishment of Tityus in black chalk	1532	Windsor, Royal Academy
D The Fall of Phaeton in black chalk	1533	Windsor, Royal Library
D Archers Shooting at a Herm in red chalk	1533	Windsor, Royal Library
D Resurrection in charcoal	1533	London, British Museum
D Self portrait with a turban, pen & ink	1533	Paris, Louvre Museum
D Head of a God in Profile in red chalk	1534	Oxford, Ashmolean Museum
D Head of a God	1534	London, British Museum
D The Dream of Human Life in black chalk	1534	London, Princes Gate Collection
D Divine Head in black chalk	1534	London, British Museum
D Back Pencil sketch for Last Judgement	1534	Florence, Casa Buonarroti

Item Description	Date	Present Location
D Drawing for Last Judgement	1534	Florence, Uffizi Museum
D Study for last Judgement,	1534	France, Bonnat Museum, Bayonne
P The Last Judgement	1536-1541	Rome, Vatican, Sistine Chapel
D Pieta in black chalk	1539	Boston, Isabella Gardner Museum
D Madonna of Silence in red chalk	1540	Private collection
D Crucifixion in black chalk	1540	London, British Museum
P Conversion of St. Paul	1542-1545	Rome, Vatican, Pauline Chapel
P Crucifixion of St. Peter	1546-1550	Rome, Vatican, Pauline Chapel
D Study for the Dome of St. Peter's in pen and black chalk	1546	France, Lille, Musee Wicar
D Pencil study for a Crucifixion	1546	London, British Museum
D Grotesque Mask in red and black chalks	1546	Windsor, Royal Library
D Cartoon for Crucifixion of St. Peter	1547	Naples, Capodimonte Museum
D Cartoon Holy Family with Saints in black chalk	1553	London, British Museum
D Holy Family with Saints, cartoon in black chalk	1553	London, British Museum
D Sketch for Venus and Cupid	1554	London, Hampton Court
D Sketches for Rondanini Pieta in black chalk	1555	Oxford, Ashmolean Museum
D Crucifixion with the Virgin and St. John in black chalk, with white pigment and grey wash	1555	London, British Museum
D Window design of Farnese Palace in black chalk	1556	Oxford, Ashmolean Museum
D Plan for San Giovanni dei Florentini in pen and black and red chalks	1559	Florence, Casa Buonarroti
D Plan of the Sforza Chapel in pen	1560	Paris, Bibliotheque Nationale
D Study of windows for Porta Pia in pen and black chalk	1561	Florence, Casa Buonarroti

Appendix E: Bibliography for Michelangelo Fans:

Books:

Baldini, Umberto, *The Sculpture of Michelangelo,* Rizzoli, New York , NY 1982.

Bartz, Gabriele, and Konig, Eberhard, *Michelangelo Buonarroti, 1475 - 1564,*
    Konemann,   Koln, Germany, 1998.

Beck, James, *Three Worlds of Michelangelo,* W. W. Norton and Company, New
    York, NY   1999.

Berti, Luciano, *Florence, the City and Its Art,* SCALA, Instituto Fotografico
    Editoriale, Florence Italy, 1979.

Boussel, Patrice, *Leonardo Da Vinci,* Konecky and Konecky, New York, NY   ?

Bramly, Serge, *Leonardo, The Artist and The Man,* Penguin Books, New York,
    NY 1994

Bull, George, *Michelangelo, A Biography,* St. Martin's Griffin, New York, NY
    1995

Bull, George, and Porter, Peter, *Michelangelo, Life, Letters and Poetry,* Oxford
    University Press, Oxford, England, 1987.

Burroughs, Betty, *Vasari's Lives of the Artists,* Abridged and Edited, Simon and
    Schuster, New York, NY, 1946.

Clements, Robert, J., *Michelangelo, A Self Portrait,* Prentice-Hall, Inc.,
    Englewood Cliffs, NJ 1963.

Cleugh, James, *The Medici,* Dorset Press, New York, NY 1990

Cole, Allison, *The Renaissance,* Dorling Kindersley, New York, NY 1994

Cole, Bruce, *Italian Art 1250 - 1550,* Harper and Row, Publishers, New York, NY
    1987

Condivi, Ascanio, *The Life of Michelangelo,* Translated by Alice Sedgwick Wohl, Edited by Helmut Wohl, 2nd Edition, Pennsylvania State University Press, University park, PA 1999.

Copplestone, Trewin, *Michelangelo,* Regency House Publishing, New York, NY 1998

Coughlin, Robert, *The World of Michelangelo 1475 - 1564,* Time-Life Books, New York, NY 1966

Tolnay, Charles, *Michelangelo, Sculpture, Painter, Architect,* Princeton University Press, Princeton, NJ 1975

de Vecchi, Pierluigi, *Michelangelo,* Konecky and Konecky, New York, NY 1990.

Durant, Will, *The Renaissance; A History of Civilization in Italy from 1304 to 1576 AD,* Simon and Schuster, New York, NY 1953

Eimerl, Sarel, *The World of Giotto,* Time-Life Books, Time Incorporated, New York, NY. 1967.

Goldscheider, Ludwig, *Michelangelo, Paintings, Sculptures, Architecture,* 4 th Edition, Phaidon Publishers, Inc., Greenwich, CT 1962

Hale, John, R., Editor, *The Encyclopaedia of the Italian Renaissance,* Thames and Hudson Limited, London, 1981

Hartt, Frederick, *Art, A History of Painting, Sculpture, Architecture,* 3 rd Edition, Prentice-Hall, Inc., Englewood Cliffs, New Jersey and Harry N. Abrams, Inc., New York, NY 1989.

Hartt, Frederick, *History of Italian Renaissance Art, Painting, Sculpture and Architecture,* 3 rd edition, Harry N. Abrams, Inc. New York, NY 1987

Hartt, Frederick, *Michelangelo,* Harry N. Abrams, New York, NY 1984

Hartt, Frederick, *Michelangelo, The Complete Sculpture,* Harry N. Abrams, Inc., Publishers, New York, NY 1968.

Hibbard, Howard, *Michelangelo*, 2nd Edition, Harper and Row, Publishers, New York, NY 1974.

Hibbard, Howard, *Michelangelo, Painter, Sculpture, Architect*, The Vendome Press, New York, NY 1975

Hibbert, Christopher, *The House of Medici: Its Rise and Fall*, Morrow Quill, New York, NY 1980

Hirst, Michael, and Dunkerton, Jill, *Making and Meaning, The Young Michelangelo*, National Gallery Publications, London, 1994

Holmes, George, *The Oxford History of Italy*, Oxford University Press, Oxford, England 1997.

Hughes, Anthony, *Michelangelo*, Phaidon Press Limited, London 1997

Jestaz, Bertrand, *Architecture of the Renaissance from Brunelleschi to Palladio*, Harry N. Abrams, New York, NY 1996

Jung-Inglessis, Eva Marie, *Saint Peter's*, SCALA Books, Florence, Italy 1980.

Kelder, Diane, *Pageant of The Renaissance*, Frederick A. Preager, Publishers, New York, NY 1969.

Lemaifre, Alain and Lessing, Erich, *Florence and The Renaissance*, Finest SA/Pierre Terrail Editions, Paris 1992

Levy, Michael, *Florence, A Portrait*, Harvard University Press, Cambridge, MA 1966

Mariani, Valerio, *Michelangelo, The Painter*, Harry N. Abrams, Inc. New York, NY 1964

Martindale, Andrew, *Man and The Renaissance*, McGraw-Hill Book Company, New York, NY 1966.

McCarthy, Mary, *The Stones of Florence*, Harcourt Brace Janovich, New York, NY 1959

Mc Donald, Jesse, *Michelangelo,* Grange Books, Kent, England, 1998.

Murray, Linda and Murray, Peter, *The Art of the Renaissance*, Oxford University
    Press, New York, NY 1963

Murray, Linda, *Michelangelo, His Life, Works and Times,* Thames and Hudson,
    New York, NY 1984.

Murray, Linda, *Michelangelo,* Thames and Hudson, New York, NY 1980.

Nardini, Bruno, *Michelangelo, Biography of a Genius,* translated by Catherine
    Frost, Giunti Gruppo Editoriale, Florence, 1999.

Partridge, Loran, *The Art of Renaissance Rome, 1400 - 1600,* Harry N. Abrams,
    Inc., New York, NY 1996.

Paoletti, John T. and Radke, Gary M., *Art in Renaissance Italy,* Harry N. Abrams,
    Inc., New York, NY 1997

Plumb, J. H., *The Italian Renaissance,* Houghton, Mifflin Company, Boston, MA
    1961.

Plumb, J. H., *The Horizon Book of The Italian Renaissance,* Richard M. Ketchum,
    Editor, American Heritage Publishing, Company, Inc., New York, NY
1961.

Ross, Nicholas, *Art in Focus: Florence,* Little, Brown and Company, Boston, MA
    1995.

Ragghianti, Carlo Ludovico, Editor, *Uffizi,Florence,* Newsweek, Inc., New York,
    NY 1968.

Richmond, Robin, *Michelangelo and the Creation of the Sistine Chapel*, Crescent
    Books, New York, NY 1999

Rolland, Romain, *Michelangelo,* Albert and Charles Boni, Inc. France, 1935.

Sala, Charles, *Michelangelo, Sculptor, Painter, Architect,* Finest SA/Pierre Terrail
    Editions, Paris 1995.

Salmi, Mario, *The Complete Work of Michelangelo,* Reynal and Company and William Morrow and Company, New York, NY 1964.

Seeley, E. L., *Lives of the Artists from Giorgio Vasari,* Selected and Edited, The Noonday Press, Inc., New York, NY 1957

Stone, Irving, *The Story of Michelangelo's Pieta,* Double Day and Company, Inc., Garden City, NY 1964.

Stone, Irving, *The Agony and The Ecstasy, A Novel of Michelangelo,* Doubleday and Company, Inc., Garden City, NY 1961 (See also the movie by the same title)

Symonds, John Addington, *The Life of Michelangelo Buonarroti,* Modern Library, New York, NY   ?

Towan, Rolf, *The Art of The Italian Renaissance,* Konemann, Koln, Germany, 1995.

Turner, Richard, A., *Renaissance Florence: The Invention of a New Art,* Harry N. Abrams, Inc., New York, NY 1997.

Vasari, Giorgio, *Lives of Seventy of the Most Eminent Painters, Sculptors and Architects,* Edited and annotated by E. H. Blashfield, E. W. Blashfield and A. A. Hopkins, (in four volumes) based on Mrs. Foster's translation completed in 1850, Charles Scribner's Sons, New York, NY 1902.

****** *The Vatican Collections: The Papacy and Art,* The Metropolitan Museum of Art, New York, Harry N. Abrams, Inc., Publishers, New York, NY 1982.

Venturi, Lionello and Skira-Venturi, Rosabianca, *Italian Painting: The Creators of the Renaissance,* translated by Stuart Gilbert, Albert Skira, Geneva, 1950.

Vollmer, Emil, *Leonardo Da Vinci,* Reynal and Company, New York, NY 1956

Wadley, Nicholas, *Michelangelo,* Spring Books, London, 1965.

Wallace, Robert, *The World of Leonardo,* Time-Life Books, Time Incorporated, New York 1966.

Wallace, William E., *Michelangelo: The Complete Sculpture, Painting, Architecture.* Hugh Lauter Levin Associates, Inc. Beaux Arts Editions. New York, 1998.

Videos:

Grubin, David, *The Power of the Past: Florence*, PBS Home Video, Washington, DC, 1996, 90 minutes

Labella, Vincenzo, *A Season of Giants*, RAI Productions in Association with Turner Pictures Consolidated Ltd., Telepool GMBH, RAI Radiotelevisione, Italiana, 1991, 4 hours

Rekant, Stuart B., *Michelangelo: Artist and Man.* Biography Series from Arts and Entertainment, A & E Television Networks and Non Fiction Films, Inc. New York, NY 1999   50 minutes

Snyder, Robert and Sonnabend, Michael, *Michelangelo, Self Portrait,* Masters and Masterworks, Sebastapol, CA 1989 (a remake of the 1951 film) 85 minutes.

Snyder, Robert and Sonnabend, Michael, *The Titan, Story of Michelangelo,* Masters and Masterworks, Sebastapol, CA 1951 (Academy Award Winner for Best Documentary) 60 minutes.

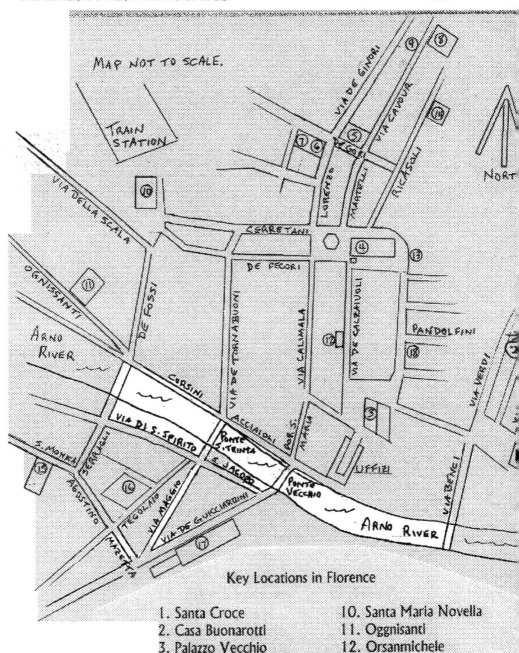

Key Locations in Florence

1. Santa Croce
2. Casa Buonarotti
3. Palazzo Vecchio
4. Duomo (Cathedral)
5. Palazzo Ricardi
6. San Lorenzo
7. Medici Library
8. San Marco
9. Site of Medici Garden
10. Santa Maria Novella
11. Oggnisanti
12. Orsanmichele
13. Museo del Opera
14. Accademia di Belle Arti
15. Santa Maria del Carmine
16. Santo Spirito
17. Palazzo Pitti
18. Bargello

Drawn by C. Washington

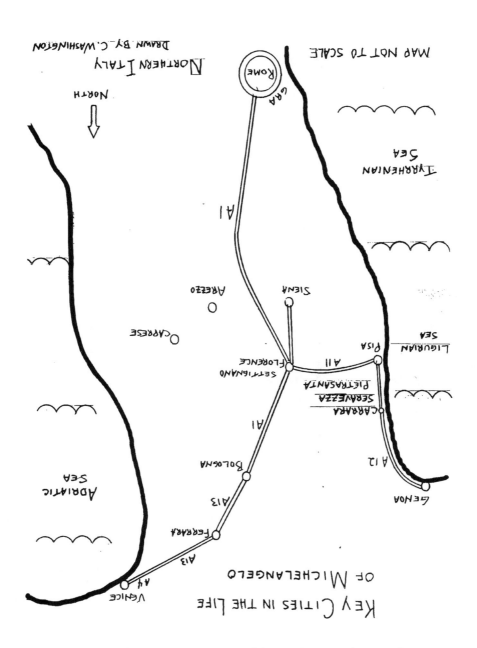

Key Cities in the Life
of Michelangelo

Northern Italy

Drawn By: C. Washington

North

MAP NOT TO SCALE

Order Form for signed copies of
Michelangelo: In the Footsteps of the Master

Advantage Publishing
~~P. O. Box 881~~
~~Fort Collins, CO 80522~~
Phone: 970-226-5493
Fax: 970-225-0259
e-mail: chuckwashingtonace@msn.com

Advantage Publishing
1125 Deercroft Ct.
Fort Collins, CO 80525
(970) 226-5493 Fax(970) 225-0259

Send_____copies of *Michelangelo* @ $16 each
plus shipping and handling to

_____
Name

_____
Address

_____
City, State, ZIP

Shipping and Handling:
1. Add $3 for 1st book in USA and $4 for Canada and Mexico.
2. Add $1 for each additional book in USA and $2 for Canada
    and Mexico.
3. Add $9 for 1st book overseas airmail, $6 for each additional
    book overseas.

Payment:
Check or Money Order in US$_____
Make payable to Advantage Publishing.

Indicate if a special message is to be inscribed.